Portraits of Greatness
YOUSUF KARSH

Thomas Nelson & Sons

THOMAS NELSON AND SONS LTD
LONDON AND EDINBURGH

THOMAS NELSON AND SONS LTD
JOHANNESBURG
MELBOURNE

SOCIÉTÉ FRANÇAISE D'ÉDITIONS NELSON
PARIS

THOMAS NELSON AND SONS
NEW YORK

FIRST PRINTED IN 1959
REPRINTED 1960, 1961

To Solange

who shared my hope and faith
and helped me to find the light

•

CONTENTS

Introduction, 11

INTRODUCTION

The aim and the art of the portraitist who works with a camera are not merely to produce a likeness but to reveal the mind and the soul behind the human face. When I have had the opportunity of studying those who have left their mark upon our time, I have tried to focus my camera on that quality which has made my subjects stand out from among their contemporaries. I have always been in quest of a secret, for that quality is elusive, indefinable.

Often, in my experience with distinguished subjects, I have wondered whether the great possess any traits in common. It is my conclusion that they do indeed share certain traits. The physical details of the faces of artists and thinkers vary, of course, but anyone who examines these portraits will observe in them all, I think, an inward power, the power that is essential to any work of the mind or imagination. In all my subjects I indeed expected to find evidence of such power and I was not disappointed. But these faces often bear too the marks of struggle, of the reach that always exceeds the grasp—and sometimes in them is the loneliness of the explorer. They also bear, or so it seems to me, the trace of the fierce competition characteristic of human affairs in our era; sometimes the gleam of arrogance; always the sign of the uncertainty and ceaseless search for truth which, you might say, are the hallmark of the thoughtful man confronted by the dilemma of his species as it is presented today.

The fascination of photography has never ceased for me. But perhaps the fascination of the human face in its inexhaustible subtlety is even greater. The portraits in this book represent years of work and unceasing experiment, and also some luck. Only in a space of time far too short for measurement does a man fully express himself, and then unconsciously—by the glint of an eye, a sudden change of mood, a casual but deeply significant gesture of the hand. Except in such magic interludes, the mask of daily life conceals; the curtain we all wear before the world is rolled down. There is thus always a revealing moment, a moment of truth, which, if lost, may never be recaptured. The photographer must learn to evoke it, to sense it, to be ready for it when it makes its fleeting appearance. Otherwise the moment of truth passes, and the chance to record the real man passes also.

Success requires, of course, the utmost concentration, but that concentration must never be allowed to show. The sitter must be made to feel at ease and yet, if he is to be portrayed truthfully, he must also be alert, at his best; his personality must expand under the brilliance of the lights and thus register fully on the film.

These are the occupational hazards of the portraitist working with the camera and often they must defeat him. How far I have succeeded in overcoming such obstacles, the viewer of these pictures must judge for himself. I have tried to reduce the hazards by making it my practice to prepare myself mentally for a sitting by searching out any information on my subject which will enable me to respond to his personality more easily on our meeting. I try to familiarize myself with his interests and hobbies, and to read all I can about him, to learn something of the career which he has made. I have no pre-conceived idea of how I will photograph any subject, and this gathering of information has often been of great benefit in making a sitting an exercise of enjoyable and revealing conversation in which anecdote, discussion, question and answer have mingled to assist me in 'discovering' the subject, visually and emotionally. The reader will overhear some of this conversation by means of the prose profiles which accompany the portraits, and in them too he will sometimes be a sharer in conversations continued later by means of correspondence.

When I came to assemble from my collection the portraits which I wished to include in this book, I discovered that it was greatness and humanity as exhibited in certain kinds of people to which I have responded with most warmth and excitement. The reader will be aware of this as he watches the gallery of artists, composers, scientists, musicians, actors, writers, and philosophers of either past history or present affairs; it does not include politicians as such—Mr. Eisenhower appears as a leader of men in war, Mr. Pearson as a leader of men seeking peace.

Like any craftsman, I am far from satisfied with my work, but I hope that the viewer of this gallery of portraits gathered over a long time and a wide area will agree that the face of talent and thought at this most puzzling point in history is one full of interest, of perception, success and failure, and incommunicable dreams. If the past is legible upon it, so, in however vague a fashion, is the future, since these men and women, and their kind everywhere, are moulding the mind of the world.

The search for genuine greatness, as distinguished from ephemeral notoriety, and the compelling passion to capture it, have been both a burden and a boon to me. They have been a burden because they have driven me to work harder than I ever intended to work. They have urged me to strive for perfection knowing it to be unattainable, and have often brought frustration and agony when the highest expression somehow escaped me at the very moment when it seemed most possible. Yet my quest has also been a boon in that it has brought me great joy, springing in those times when something close to the ideal has been attained. It has kept me young in heart, adventurous, growing perhaps, and forever seeking. It has taken me close to so many remarkable people around the world that I have never regretted a moment of my time or a mile of my travels. I speak with some experience when I say that I have rarely left the company of accomplished men and women without feeling that they had in them real sincerity, integrity—yes, sometimes vanity of course—and always a sense of high purpose.

Yet after this frequent roaming I always come back to Canada, the country of my free choice and adoption, my true homeland. I venture to think that it is a good thing for the world that men of other countries and from far places are coming to North America, just as North Americans are travelling more and more abroad. For such journeys to end in the meeting of many of the world's leaders face to face—therein, I believe, lies the hope of a better day: for you do not know a man merely by report, only by looking into his eyes and listening to his words.

Here, in these pages, are some portraits of the gifted, the harvest of a long search. I hope they may bring my subjects a little closer to those who view them, and that they convey something of the intellect, the emotional struggle, the pride and prejudice, the will power, the love, and the doubts of our time.

Acknowledgment is made of courteous permission for quotation of passages from: *Reflections on the Cinema* by René Clair, translated by Vera Traill (William Kimber and Company Limited; Librairie Gallimard); *Our New Music: Leading Composers in Europe and America* by Aaron Copland (McGraw-Hill Book Company, Inc.); *What to Listen for in Music* by Aaron Copland (rev. ed.; McGraw-Hill Book Company, Inc., 1957); *Music and Imagination* by Aaron Copland (Harvard University Press); "My Conception of Hell" by Gian Carlo Menotti, in *Saturday Review of Literature*, XXXIII (April 22, 1950); "'That's Georgia'" by Anita Pollitzer, in *Saturday Review of Literature*, XXXIII (November 4, 1950); *America and Alfred Stieglitz: A Collective Portrait* by Waldo Frank *et al.* (Doubleday, Doran & Company, Inc.)

KONRAD ADENAUER

Chancellor since 1949 of the Federal Republic of Germany. Born in 1876; twice widowed; has seven children; devout Roman Catholic. Educated at Freiburg, Munich, and Bonn Universities; practised law in Cologne. Lord Mayor of Cologne, 1917-33; member of provincial Diet of Rhine Province, 1917-33; President of Prussian State Council, 1920-33. Dismissed from official duties in 1933. Member of British Zone Advisory Council, 1946-9; President of Parliamentary Council of three Western Zones, 1948-9. Honorary degrees from many universities.

The German whom Churchill has called the greatest of his race since Bismarck could best be understood, it seemed logical to suppose, in his own surroundings. For that reason I travelled all the way to Bonn, in 1954, but was unable to photograph Konrad Adenauer there. A photographer cannot always choose his setting. As it turned out, I focused my camera on this extraordinary man in the house of a friend at Greenwich, Connecticut, in 1955. ~ The West German Chancellor had received an honorary degree that morning from Harvard University. He was obviously tired, typically uncommunicative, but friendly and receptive. I have no German and he offered no English. Though we might have broken the barrier of language in French, he clearly preferred silence. ~ The silence seemed to me more instructive than words. A sense of power clung to him like a garment, and it required no utterance. The square-cut and deeply graven face, the huge body, and, above all, the sombre granitic look indicated a singleness of purpose, a dedication to some inward and unshakable decision. ~ His public decisiveness, the basis of his political career, is, of course, well known. This man had become the master of his people; he had brought them back to the family of Western nations and he was determined to save them from a communist doctrine not only dangerous politically, but, to him, inherently anti-Christian and evil. ~ He has, I suspect, that rare genius of common sense—the instinct for the workable thing—which the Germans, for all their instinct for practicality in other fields, had long abandoned in international affairs, with tragic results. Yet he is driven on by his own dream, the dream of a better Germany. He had suffered much for that dream under Hitler and the suffering was legible on his face. It showed the firmness achieved only from suffering, the self-assurance of his undoubted success, and the subtlety and wariness of Der Alte (the Old One), as his people like to call him. There was also a certain disillusionment and stark loneliness. He seemed, in short, the image, as a sculptor might have carved it in rough stone, of a lost people who were finding themselves. In stone, yes. For this man appeared ageless and indestructible. ~ I watched him intently, hoping that for one unguarded moment he might reveal himself. Presently he rested his head on his hand like a weary man oblivious to others and engulfed in his own thoughts. The moment had come, and I committed it to my film.

MARIAN ANDERSON

One of the world's leading contraltos. She was born in Philadelphia and as a child sang in her Baptist church choir. A fund raised through a church concert enabled her to take singing lessons under an Italian teacher. In 1925 came public recognition of her talent, when out of 300 she won first prize in a competition in New York. During the last thirty years she has made many concert tours in the United States and Europe. Appointed member of the United States delegation to the United Nations and a member of the U.N. Trusteeship Committee, 1958.

The world knows the voice of Marian Anderson. It has enriched our music, and through it has been made eloquent the long tragedy of the Negro race and her own triumph over it. ~ This realization is for all who hear and see her. What struck me most, however, when I photographed her at her home in Connecticut in 1945, was her simplicity and peacefulness. With her, I was convinced, the harmony of music came from the harmony of her being. The Negro spirituals which have deeply moved us all are not merely the result of a glorious voice and long technical training; they utter her own nature. ~ My problem was to capture and register this quality —not an easy problem even when she fell in with my suggestions with almost childlike obedience. None of my early shots satisfied me in the least. All of them, I felt, had missed the intangible target. I began to despair. Then, towards the conclusion of the sitting, Miss Anderson's accompanist came in for a rehearsal. This seemed to be my chance. I asked him, in a whisper, to play very softly the accompaniment to 'The Crucifixion,' one of the singer's favourite compositions. Unaware of my innocent little plot, she began to hum to herself. Hurriedly, I snapped the camera. When I developed and printed the film I felt that it contained what I had seen with my own eyes. This is the portrait of a harmonious soul revealing itself unconsciously in song. ~ Later, this picture was exhibited at the Museum of Modern Art in New York. A man who saw it there told me afterwards that it had brought tears to his eyes because he remembered his own moving experience with Miss Anderson. He had been one of eleven people invited to her birthday party at her home, 'Mariana Farm,' in Connecticut. Before the guests partook of a light meal, her mother suggested to Miss Anderson that she sing 'The Lord's Prayer.' 'We always say grace before a meal,' the mother explained. As the daughter sang grace that day there were few dry eyes among her listeners. ~ I could understand this after I had studied the Negro singer for myself. She speaks to us, above the clash of race, in the language of all humanity.

JEAN-LOUIS BARRAULT

French actor, director, and producer; an outstanding mime. Born 1910. From 1940 to 1946 he was with the Comédie Française as producer-director; afterwards he formed his own company with Madeleine Renaud, his wife, at the Marigny Theatre, Paris. He has toured Britain, Western Europe, Canada, the United States, and South America and has made several films, including Les Enfants du Paradis, D'hommes à hommes *and* La Ronde.

The setting for this portrait of a famous member of the modern school of acting in France struck me, at first glance, as the most hopeless I had ever encountered. Yet it turned out to be ideal for my purpose. ∼ I had climbed to the upper part of the Marigny Theatre, in Paris, where Jean-Louis Barrault was playing in 1949. Everything behind the scenes seemed to be in that pandemonium which only the hard-headed French can achieve. It was difficult to find any sort of suitable background, much less a prop—and this in a theatre! When I seized a chair from a roped-off enclosure and asked Barrault to sit on it, the female owner of the theatre engaged me in a violent duel of French words. Somehow I won that skirmish and my subject sank gratefully into the chair. ∼ Now I realized that my troubles were only beginning. M. Barrault is a difficult man to photograph: alert, moody, puckish, and highly nervous. This actor of world-wide reputation never knew, he said, what to do with his hands and complained that they 'froze' on him. This, I saw, was only the artist's salutary dissatisfaction with his own work. In fact, he unconsciously assumed the characteristic attitudes that I wished to record. His hands seemed to me as eloquent as his speech. ∼ As he squirmed, gesticulated, and protested against the general cussedness of things, I snapped him in motion, trying especially to catch that woebegone expression of the instinctive mime. It reminded me of Canada's wonder, Fridolin (Gratien Gélinas), and of the downtrodden but unconquerable human creature everywhere. ∼ M. Barrault was worried that day, almost frantically, about the difficulty of getting to North America, in answer to an official invitation. 'All expenses are paid, for myself and company, from the very moment we land. All that's required is for so many million francs to be transferred from one government ministry to another. But the difficulties'—he flung out his hands in desperation—'are insurmountable.' ∼ I urged him to cheer up and predicted that he would come to America and have a great success. He gave me a mime's look of infinite sadness. Then a smile broke through his gloom—the smile of the world's little man who survives everything.

THE RT. HON. WILLIAM MAXWELL AITKEN, P.C., KT.

FIRST BARON AND FIRST BARONET OF BEAVERBROOK, NEW BRUNSWICK, AND CHERKLEY, SURREY

Publisher of the London (England) Evening Standard, Sunday Express *and* Daily Express. *Born in Maple, Ontario, Canada, 1879; educated at the public school in Newcastle, New Brunswick. Entered politics in England, 1910. Special correspondent, Canadian Expeditionary Force, 1914-18; Canadian Government Representative at the Front, 1916-18; officer in charge of Canadian War Records, 1917. Chancellor, Duchy of Lancaster and Minister of Information, 1918; Minister for Aircraft Production, 1940-1; Minister of State, 1941; Minister of Supply, 1941-2; Lord Privy Seal, 1943-5. Chancellor of the University of New Brunswick, 1947-53; Honorary Chancellor, 1954.*

It would be, I expected, a formidable undertaking to photograph Lord Beaverbrook. This Canadian who has made himself one of the most influential men in modern Britain, must be, I supposed, a truly formidable person. No doubt he is, but with me, and other guests at his country home, he appeared as the personification of charm, a delightful host and a man of extraordinary candour. What was his recipe for success? 'Judgment, industry, and health. I have no ulcers and I don't intend to get any.' ~ In the background of this 1949 portrait is a carved lion, a miniature of the Landseer lions of Trafalgar Square and, as it seemed to me, an appropriate comment on Lord Beaverbrook's regnant career. Behind this household ornament there is an amusing story. ~ At his London home, 'Stornoway House,' a score of these lions formed part of the grand staircase. When the house was bombed in the last war the owner himself retrieved two of the statues from the ruins and in the confusion was arrested by a 'bobby' as a looter. The policeman would not believe that the little man with the lions in his arms was the great British publisher and statesman, until one of Lord Beaverbrook's servants arrived and offered to carry this heavy freight. It amazed me to hear that anyone in Britain would not recognize the famous face of 'the Beaver,' but I soon realized on meeting him at close quarters, that he is not the man the public generally supposes. He is much more complicated, a strange mixture of the harsh and the gentle, the worldly and the unworldly. ~ We have talked, naturally, of newspapers and their public. 'First of all,' Lord Beaverbrook has remarked, 'there is a duty laid upon all papers without exception to tell the news truthfully, regardless of whether it suits the prejudices of the public or of the editor. A newspaper proprietor who lowered his standards or altered his aims to suit the supposed views of the public would be contemptible and not likely to succeed. For the public is not without perception in detecting insincerity. A proprietor would not expect to succeed if his views ran too violently against popular opinion, or were unskilfully conveyed. A newspaper seeks to persuade. It requires a talent for advocacy, but all this is subject to the overriding necessity of giving a faithful account of world and domestic affairs. ~ About the Commonwealth, he said: 'The British Commonwealth, or Empire as I prefer to call it, has been greatly weakened by foolish policies and the failure to pursue constructive and wise ones. The rebuilding of the Empire's influence is a clamant need of the age. None of the international agencies developed in competition with the Empire shows the slightest signs of taking over from it the functions which it used to discharge. Recovery from this situation calls for long views, patience and determination.'

SIR THOMAS BEECHAM, BT., C.H.

British conductor and operatic director. Born in 1879, he succeeded his father, the first baronet, in 1916. Made his début with the Queens Hall Orchestra, London; founded the Beecham Symphonic Orchestra and Beecham Opera Company; reorganized the Royal Philharmonic Society, its conductor 1945-. Has made many tours; in the United States has conducted the New York Philharmonic Symphony Orchestra and at the Metropolitan Opera. Has promoted operatic and ballet seasons at London's Covent Garden. His second wife, whom he married in 1943, was Betty Humby, the concert pianist.

It was not with alarm but with a firm resolve that in 1946 I approached Sir Thomas Beecham, the elderly *enfant terrible* of the musical world. I remembered his concert, a few years previously in Ottawa, when his temper and frequent hissing had annoyed me greatly, and I had made up my mind that I would order my assistant to pack up and would be ready to withdraw immediately if Sir Thomas proved in the least fiery. ~ He greeted me at the door of his New York hotel suite in his dressing gown with the announcement that he would be leaving in a few hours for an extended tour. This sounded ominous, but as it happened I had no reason to fear the great tyrant over audiences. Sir Thomas turned out to be a polished gentleman, full of suavity and anecdotes. By the time my equipment was set up and the lights ready, so was he, perfectly groomed, as gentle as a dove. ~ His charm and my surprise continued until I asked him if he arranged his own music for his orchestra. That question produced an instant explosion. 'Do you think,' he demanded, 'I would leave such important work to nincompoops?' There followed a long string of vigorous adjectives: 'malaprop' and 'addle-pated' I remember among the elegant terms of abuse. Clearly no one but Beecham could arrange Beecham's orchestrations. I went on with my work. ~ Sir Thomas soon recovered his calm and suggested that I include in the photographs the clock always kept on his working desk. This seemed a sound idea. The clock might symbolize his promptitude and meticulous attention to detail. (I remembered the famous story of the Covent Garden concert at which he belaboured the London aristocracy for coming in late.) ~ So we included the clock. As I left him I felt that I had met the puckish conductor at his best. His glistening eyes, ready wit, and razor-edged mind had made the sitting a delight.

CHARLES HERBERT BEST, C.B.E.

Canadian physiologist; co-discoverer of insulin with Sir Frederick Banting (in the laboratory of Professor J. J. R. Macleod), 1921. Banting assigned Best equal credit for the discovery and divided his share of the Nobel Prize with him (1923). Born 1899; educated at the Universities of Toronto and London. Professor of Physiology and Head of the Department at the University of Toronto since 1929; Director, Banting and Best Department of Medical Research since 1941. A Scientific Director, International Health Division, Rockefeller Foundation, 1941-43, 1946-48. During World War II initiated Canadian project for securing dried human serum for military use (1939); joined Royal Canadian Navy as Director, Medical Research Unit (1941) and with his colleagues made many practical contributions to the safety and efficiency of naval personnel. Initiated work which led to purification of heparin and clinical use as first antithrombotic agent. Discovered new enzyme system and, with his colleagues, a new vitamin. Has received many decorations and honorary degrees.

The great Canadian medical man and co-discoverer of insulin does not strike one as a scientist—until he begins to talk. Dr. Best is an informal person, readily and instantly liked. He is, of course, an indefatigable worker, in the University of Toronto's Charles Best Institute, where I photographed him in 1958 in his laboratory, as well as a lecturer, a traveller, and, I would guess, what the English call an 'enjoying man.' He is also completely dedicated to his work of improving the life of mankind. ~ When I put a series of questions to him about his own field, his replies were quick and business-like, yet full of suggestion. The discovery of insulin, he told me, had not occurred by any chance or wild surmise. It had been a systematic process. The late Sir Frederick Banting and he had set out to find a substance in pancreas which would eliminate the fatal diabetes which develops in de-pancreatized dogs. Dr. Best admitted, however, that chance often played an important part in research, although usually it was only the well-trained researcher who recognized the opportunity before him. New ideas sometimes arose from reading, from departmental seminars, group discussions, and debates between individuals. There were two types of research workers, both useful in their own fields—the 'explorers' and the 'developers.' Though he didn't say so, I guessed that Dr. Best and Sir Frederick had been both. Nowadays Dr. Best devotes himself mostly to the supervision of younger colleagues, and gives suggestions to more senior men if they are requested. ~ There was no shortage of excellent research workers in his institution, he said. Did over-specialization endanger research? No, not in medicine. He and his associates, he added, were now working on many different diseases. ~ The most important contribution to medical knowledge in the last ten years, he said without hesitation, was the study of the chemical basis of heredity. ~ I had ventured as a layman to suggest that when one remedy for a human illness is discovered it often seems to start another pest into operation, as if a mysterious attack and counter-attack were under way in the body. 'Not so,' said Dr. Best crisply. 'The top of a new mountain reveals vistas of great beauty and many previously unknown chasms.' ~ Few men have seen more of this awesome scenery than the amiable doctor.

ALFRED BLALOCK

Professor of surgery at The Johns Hopkins University, Baltimore, Maryland, and surgeon-in-chief at The Johns Hopkins Hospital since 1941. Born in 1899; studied at Georgia University and Johns Hopkins University School of Medicine. From 1925 to 1941 held appointments at Vanderbilt University Hospital and Vanderbilt University, Pennsylvania; then returned to Johns Hopkins. Has received medical awards from many countries in recognition of his contribution to thoracic surgery.

It is not easy to photograph Dr. Alfred Blalock, the surgeon who, with Dr. Helen Taussig, perfected the operation on 'blue babies.' In 1950 he was about to perform his thousandth 'blue baby' operation and his colleagues had commissioned me to commemorate the event, but the surgeon, I was told, would take a great deal of persuading. As one of his associates explained to me, he could be enticed before my camera only with an innocent subterfuge. I was to tell him that, in the interests of his profession, he must be included in my gallery of scientists. ~ Thus warned, I waited until his programme was a little lighter than usual, telephoned him, and made an appointment. We spent a lively evening together. At dinner, by way of discovering his personality, I talked freely about doctors and remarked rather brashly that in the main they were very vain creatures. He took this in good part and suggested that, if I were interested in his profession, I had better see a 'blue baby' operation for myself. ~ Accordingly, I was amazed and not a little nervous to find myself in an operating room next morning, wearing a mask and gown and standing at the left hand of the surgeon. Then, for two hours, he applied the magic of his mind and fingers to the body of a child seven years old. ~ I was awed by Dr. Blalock's dexterity and more by his calm. He proceeded easily and naturally, often talked to me with no sign of tension, and explained his methods to visiting doctors from many parts of the world who sat in the operating amphitheatre. As time wore on I lost my awe and two hours stretched into eternity. Since I could not understand the operation, all my thoughts were on that life under the scalpels. There was no need to worry. Nothing disturbed Dr. Blalock. He finished his incredible task on schedule, ordered the patient wheeled out of the operating room, and removed his gloves like a man who has done an ordinary morning's work. ~ He might then have turned to the 'Coke' and the cigarette which are his constant companions, but his single thought was for the mother of the child. Before he had even removed his gown, he went to a telephone and assured this anxious woman that the operation was successful. His telephone conversation, more than his skill, told me what sort of man I was going to photograph. And I hastened to say: 'Dr. Blalock, I take back everything I said last night about the vanity of doctors. If you have such a thing, which I doubt, you are more than entitled to it.'

NIELS BOHR

Danish physicist. Born 1885; educated at the University of Copenhagen. Lecturer at the Universities of Copenhagen (1913) and Manchester (1914-16); Professor of Theoretical Physics, University of Copenhagen, since 1916; Director of the Institute for Theoretical Physics, Copenhagen, since 1920. In 1939 brought news of the cracking of the uranium atom to New York. Awarded, among many decorations, Nobel Prize in Physics, 1922, and first Atoms for Peace Award, 1957.

When I came to photograph Dr. Bohr in 1958 at the Institute for Advanced Study (in the same Princeton office previously occupied by Albert Einstein) I met one of the world's leading atomic scientists, also a dreamer, and a man who liked to ponder every question thoroughly and answer at length, often in homely parables. ~ With a humorous glint in his eye, and nursing his precious pipe, he greeted me warmly, but remarked: 'I'm diffident about being photographed by you. You have portrayed so many legendary people.' 'It's for the same reason,' I said, 'that I'm here to photograph you.' ~ I asked him how he felt when he unlocked the secret of atomic structure—like a climber conquering Mount Everest? He did not answer directly but told me of a mountaineer who had reached a height eighty feet from the top of a high mountain and could go no further. But this man was determined to try again, so that he could tell his children he had succeeded. 'That,' said the mountaineer's friend, 'should be the best reason not to repeat the adventure.' ~ I had to be satisfied with this oblique reply. He was more specific when I wondered whether the Western world would produce more scientific genius if it spent more money on research. 'This talk we hear,' he mused, 'so much of it is stupid. What we need is genius among politicians, coupled with a measure of humour.' ~ Is it not true, I ventured to ask, that some scientists prefer not to assign to Almighty God a role in our lives? 'Well,' said Dr. Bohr, 'Almighty is a word so encompassing. Things are relative and they have to equate.' Then he launched into another parable—the story of three ancient Greek philosophers who first tasted vinegar. One pronounced it sour, the next bitter, and the third fresh. 'So you see,' Dr. Bohr chuckled, 'everything is comparative and means something different to different people.' ~ Turning to more practical things, he asserted his belief that world-wide scientific co-operation was humanity's best hope, since knowledge held the keys to understanding. ~ Then came sentences I shall not forget. 'I'm interested,' he said, 'in mercy and compassion. I'm interested in beauty that can't be expressed in words or pictures, music or mathematics.' I remembered his oft-repeated statement to his students: 'Every sentence I utter must be understood not as an affirmation, but as a question.' But there seemed no question, only affirmation, here.

GEORGES BRAQUE

French painter, sculptor, and engraver who is renowned as an exponent of classical cubism. Born in 1882, Braque first exhibited at the Salon d'Automne and Salon des Indépendants in 1905. Since then he has frequently exhibited at galleries in and out of France. His works are represented in the Museum of Modern Art, New York; the Tate Gallery, London; and the Musée National d'Art Moderne, Paris.

All his life Georges Braque, the French painter, has been preoccupied with space. With extraordinary imagination and his own unique methods he has painted space, and his work, with that of Picasso, is said to have had the greatest influence on modern painting. ~ His house in Paris was in complete disarray when I went to photograph him in 1949, the tiny living room almost empty and its furniture heaped up as if for moving day. We went upstairs to his studio and prepared to make his portrait. ~ M. Braque seemed a little surprised, almost disappointed, that I did not wish to portray him with some of his paintings in the background. This type of photograph, I said, had been rather overdone of late. I had come to picture the man, not his work. I did use one prop—a 'casquette,' a cloth cap of his own design, made for him in both black and white. It suited him well in either colour. ~ M. Braque was a delightful man, innocent of all pretence. A jovial subject, he was much more approachable for me than his cubist pictures which I confess I had vainly studied before I visited him. I enjoyed his company.

30

BENJAMIN BRITTEN, C.H.

British composer. Born at Lowestoft, 1913; studied at the Royal College of Music, and afterwards privately with musicians Frank Bridge and Harold Samuel. Since then has devoted his time to composing and concert-giving, the latter mostly with Peter Pears, well-known tenor. Musical Director of the English Opera Group, 1947; founded Aldeburgh Festival (in Suffolk), 1948. Among his operas are Peter Grimes, The Rape of Lucretia, Albert Herring, Billy Budd, Gloriana *(composed for the Coronation of Queen Elizabeth II in 1953),* Turn of the Screw *and* Noye's Fludde.

Every circumstance conspired against my attempt to photograph Benjamin Britten in 1954. The brilliant British composer lives in a tiny kingdom of his own at Aldeburgh, in the County of Suffolk, and my driver lost his way to our appointment. Mr. Britten was irritated at my lateness, insisted he must play a regular set of tennis to exercise a lame right arm and, then, when my camera was set up, leaped into the sea, which comes right up to his house. That plunge cooled him off remarkably and we got on well together after that. ∼ Some time later, in direct answer to questions, he illuminated for me aspects of contemporary music, especially his own. ∼ The great disadvantage suffered by contemporary opera in Britain, he said, was the shortage of opera houses, and the reluctance of the public to accept anything new or out of the way. ∼ He denied my suggestion that all his operas were sombre, if not tragic, in atmosphere. Some of his most successful works were comic or at least cheerful, he insisted. ∼ I remarked that he had worked a good deal with the English Opera Group and with Peter Pears in particular. When writing, did he have particular people in mind? 'It's always a great inspiration,' he said, 'to work for particular artists. One gets stimulus from knowing their personal characteristics, though a disadvantage is that it makes the artists difficult to replace.' ∼ When I asked him why the words for most of his songs had been written by major poets, he told me that he read an enormous amount of poetry, naturally preferring what he considered great. 'On the whole,' he remarked, 'I choose poems lyric and not epic, succinct in form and with clear images. The music stems directly from the words, deriving from the poem's colour and rhythm as well as from its meaning. The result is certainly a new entity with its own individual life, but in no way replacing the poem in its naked form.' ∼ He has an intense interest in folk songs, which he arranges with peculiar beauty. 'The setting of folk songs presents the special problem that one has to try to absorb the songs, and try to become as if one had had the luck to have written the tune oneself. One becomes, as it were, another link in the long chain of interpreters, since the song first appeared.' ∼ Those last words strike me as happily chosen. For Benjamin Britten is himself a strong and brilliant link in the long chain of English music.

PEARL S. BUCK

American writer. Born in West Virginia but spent her girlhood in China; educated in China and at Randolph Macon College for Women and Cornell University. Later returned to China; came back to the United States in 1932; is now Advisory Editor for the John Day Company. Awarded Nobel Prize for Literature, 1938. Her publications include: House of Earth *(a trilogy),* Dragon Seed, My Several Worlds, Imperial Woman.

I had long admired Pearl Buck from a distance as a novelist who has given the Western world a new insight into the mystery of China. I met her personally in 1958 at her Pennsylvania farm, and came also to admire the great woman who is also the novelist. ∼ At my prompting, she talked for some time about the women of China, remarking that, like the women of France, they were contented because they lived in a world of their own making. They had a tolerance and set of values quite different from those of the West. It did not seem strange to them, for instance, if the man of the family maintained a 'home' wife to look after the parents, children, and servants, and a 'city wife' to entertain his business associates and acquaintances. Nor did this system of morality seem to alarm Miss Buck. Tolerance, perhaps, is the secret of her literary success. ∼ Turning to her work, she told me she always experienced two difficult periods in writing a book. The first occurred before she began, the dreadful and doubtful period of preparation when everything was amorphous and unborn: the second half way through the task, when it was too late to go back and cut down the words already written and yet the remainder could not possibly include all she wished to say. ∼ I observed that women faced special difficulties in literature, as in the other arts, being often discounted by the public and the critics merely because they were women. At this Miss Buck smiled. 'A woman,' she said, 'must remember that, though she is doing a man's job, she is still a woman.' ∼ The monuments to her womanhood, her finest monuments, are well known, though she never parades them. Near her home she and some friendly neighbours have established that Welcome House where many children of mixed blood, the most tragic victims of our society, have been given a home, an education, and, what is far more important, an affection which knows no colour line. ∼ Miss Buck told me a tender little story of a dark-skinned child whom she had adopted, quite late in her life, when most women would not think of accepting such a responsibility. One day this child came, weeping bitterly, to the only mother she knew, because her playmates had called her a 'nigger.' Miss Buck replied that as a girl in China, the daughter of a missionary, she had felt the same kind of slight, the Chinese children often treating her with contempt because she was only 'a white girl.'

RALPH JOHNSON BUNCHE

An Under-Secretary at the United Nations since 1955. Born in Detroit, 1904. Dr. Bunche graduated from Harvard and did post-doctoral work in anthropology and colonial policy. On the staff of the University of California and Howard University. With Office of Strategic Services, 1941-4. He has specialized in the administration of trustee territory, being principal director of the U.N.'s Department of Trusteeship from 1948 to 1954 and its Acting Mediator in Palestine, 1948-9, and in the study of race relations. Awarded Nobel Peace Prize in 1950.

No Negro of our time, I suppose, has achieved the worldwide eminence of Dr. Bunche. To me he has appeared as a force for peace and human welfare, as a symbol of mankind's slow conquest of racial prejudice, his striving for brotherhood. ~ This photograph was taken in 1958 in the New York building of the United Nations, whose distinguished servant he is. Despite duties that overfill his days and nights and leave him little leisure for family life, he arrived exactly on time in the lobby of the General Assembly which I had chosen for the sitting. This, as it happened, was his 28th wedding anniversary but he could not go home even to dine with his wife. ~ As I trained my lens on him we chatted about the problem which absorbs all his energies and a magnificent intelligence: that of reconciling the nations and races of the world. Education, he said, was the most potent antidote to the prejudices, fears, and bigotry that divide mankind. There was abundant evidence to prove, he added, that education in the broad sense had diminished these evils in the United States, though the task was slow and long. ~ For example, he expected that desegregation would be achieved in the next generation, would be accepted and would work. 'I believe,' he stated, 'that it is possible for all nations to understand one another to work in peace together. The four thousand or so employees of the United Nations prove that fact. Here everyone works together irrespective of colour, race, religion, or ideology. Although the world has shrunk with modern transportation, in another sense it is greatly enlarged, for all nations are growing up and demanding their place in the world. I believe that any nation which wishes independence and is capable of governing itself should have its freedom.' ~ As the world enlarged and more nations became free, he continued, more economic help for the under-developed regions would be required, and more education, but most important of all was technological help. In these fields, as in the more obvious work of peace, the United Nations was becoming more important than ever. None of the regional defence organizations nor the efforts of individual nations could take the place of the world body. ~ But in the end what mattered most was the attitude of the individual man. 'The antagonisms, prejudices, suspicions and fears that characterize contemporary relations among societies,' he said, 'are only the collective expressions of the attitudes of great numbers of individuals in those societies. If the individuals have good will and understanding, the government of the society cannot fail to reflect it.'

VANNEVAR BUSH

Eminent American administrator, electrical engineer, and scientist; President of the Carnegie Institution, Washington, 1939-55; builder of the differential analyser which solves differential equations. Born in 1890. Worked on submarine detection during World War I. Held appointments at the Massachusetts Institute of Technology, 1919-38. Director, U.S. Office of Scientific Research and Development, 1941-7. Has received scientific awards from all over the world, Officier Légion d'Honneur; Hon. K.B.E.

My first impression of Dr. Bush, the great scientist, was one of complete serenity. As he moved and talked he reminded me forcibly of the late Will Rogers; I told him so and he cheerfully admitted the resemblance. ~ This man strikes one immediately as being goodnatured, full of human understanding, and, in the strict sense of the word, simple. I was well aware that his mind had grappled successfully with the most complex of all scientific subjects, and, unlike the minds of some scientists, with the philosophic problems behind the recent discoveries of science. ~ It seemed to me that Dr. Bush has explored the outer regions of science but never forgotten that men are much more than chemistry. He has worked with atoms but never lost the common touch. He is a human being first, I think, and a scientist second. ~ When I first met Dr. Bush in 1950 at the Carnegie Institution in Washington, I asked for a brief lecture on atomic fission. To my surprise, since I know nothing of science, Dr. Bush was able to make scientific phenomena appear not so difficult to me. With his easy explanations I almost began to imagine I was grasping the mysteries. ~ In order to illustrate his lecture, he asked some of his laboratory staff to demonstrate to me their recent photographic experiments. These were a complete failure that day because the machinery immediately broke down. To tell the truth, I derived a certain malicious satisfaction from this accident, remembering the many moments of frustration when my own electronic lights had betrayed me. Accidents, I was comforted to see, afflict not only the photographer but the greatest scientists. ~ Dr. Bush, I concluded, was not a man who easily expressed his deepest thoughts in casual conversation. His geniality perhaps covers an inner shyness. But on reading one of his addresses, which he called 'The Search for Understanding,' I found that the scientist was something of a mystic: 'Science has a simple faith, which transcends utility. Nearly all men of science, all men of learning for that matter, and men of simple ways, too, have it in some form and in some degree. It is the faith that it is the privilege of man to learn to understand, that this is his mission. If we abandon that mission under stress we shall abandon it forever, for stress will not cease. Knowledge for the sake of understanding, not merely to prevail, that is the essence of our being. . . . For if we fail to struggle and fail to think beyond our petty lot, we accept a sordid role. The light of our minds tells us that there is more to life than this.' The portrait printed here was made in Dr. Bush's home in Belmont, Massachusetts, in 1958.

ALBERT CAMUS

French author and journalist; born in 1913. Studied at University of Algiers; before the outbreak of World War II was director of L'Equipe, the theatrical company. Prominent in the French Resistance movement against the Nazi occupation. Afterwards the associate founder and Editor of Combat; *now a Director of the publishing house Librairie Gallimard. Some of his publications are:* Lettres à un ami allemand, La Peste, Les Justes *(a play),* L'Homme révolté, *and* La Chute. *Awarded the Nobel Prize for Literature in 1957.*

It had been arranged that I should photograph M. Camus in his office at Gallimard, the Paris publishers, but these premises struck me as inappropriate. The French writer and thinker must be placed in his own private surroundings, from which have emerged such fine literature and provocative thinking. We repaired to his home. It was a tiny place, as if the owner cared little for anything but his work. Still, it had an atmosphere. It was a place where the man belonged. ∼ I cast my eyes around the little room, wondering where Camus did his writing. He guessed my question and answered, 'I always write standing up at a lectern.' We tried photographing him at his lectern, but although he looked very impressive the setting did not please me. Nor was I satisfied when he sat at a desk. Finally we compromised by having him sit on the desk with an air of relaxation, or at least as much relaxation as one could expect in a person so vibrant with ideas —the left-wing prophet who is strongly anti-communist, the veteran of the wartime French Resistance movement, the advocate of the 'Mediterranean tradition.' ∼ At that time, 1954, the crisis in Indo-China was nearing its *dénouement* and he talked with gloom of the tragedy there and of how France was being bled white. I asked him questions about his books and he remarked that they had been translated into many languages, even Arabic. This prompted me to inquire if he felt that growing Arab nationalism indicated the development of a new Arab empire. Probably with the experience of his own Algerian background, he replied, 'It's much too soon to say. The Arab world is barely emerging and it will take a while for it to gain any real strength.' ∼ In France I had come into contact with so many intellectuals that I could not refrain from asking how he accounted for this wealth of mind in a single country. He gave me a mischievous look. 'Do you really think,' he countered, 'that "wealth" is the right word?' And more soberly he added: 'What is more important than quantity is quality —the right direction above all. The real question is whether we are intellectually pulling together. I doubt it.' But it has seemed to me that Albert Camus at least was moving in the right direction and probably pulling many of France's ablest minds with him.

PABLO CASALS

World's most celebrated violoncellist, and a composer and conductor. Born in Catalonia, Spain, in 1876 and educated at the Municipal School of Music, Barcelona, and the Madrid Conservatoire. ~ Made his début in England in 1898; conductor of the Pau Casals Symphony Orchestra in Barcelona which he founded. In 1940 he left Spain in protest against the Franco régime and shortly after settled at Prades on the French side of the Pyrenees; since 1950 has conducted there an annual Music Festival which is attended by many famous musicians.

As I drove along the dusty road to Prades in 1954, I had the feeling that I was on pilgrimage bent. I was going to meet that great self-exile and patron saint of music, Pablo Casals. He did not disappoint me. I had never photographed a warmer or more sensitive human being. ~ We decided to take the portraits in two sessions and against two different backgrounds. The second day we moved to the old Abbey of St. Michel de Cuxa. Though partially restored, it was empty and dark. One electric light bulb was the only illumination available but happily I secured enough current for my strobe lights. No need to pose Casals. Once he had sat down with his cello, the immediate surroundings seemed to fade from his consciousness. Soon the old abbey was throbbing with the music only he can play—music of an almost unearthly quality in this dismal chamber. I hardly dared to talk or move for fear of breaking the spell. And then, as I watched the lonely figure crouched against the rough stones, a small window high above him giving this scene the look of a prison, I suddenly decided on an unusual experiment. I would photograph the musician's back. I would record, if I could, my own vivid impression of the voluntary prisoner who, on the surge of his music, had escaped not only the prison but the world. The portrait printed here perhaps suggests the immense strength, intellectual, physical and spiritual, flowing from this amazing old man. ~ After the sitting I gently returned Casals, his cello and his chair, to his exceedingly small home (really the porter's lodge of an estate) where he invited me into his study for sherry and biscuits. So far as I could see, he had only one frailty in his eightieth year. The sun, or strong light, he said, gave him terrible headaches, and he never went about without his faded red umbrella. ~ I asked him to name the great living composers. 'Very difficult to say,' he replied, 'for me, perhaps Bloch, Enesco and Salazar.' Would any contemporary composer in years to come rank with the classical figures of music? 'I don't know,' he said, 'but I don't believe there is such a genius alive today. For me, classical music is to be adopted, felt, recognized and loved. Modern music has turned towards non-music. Though they have a natural understanding of music, the moderns reject the classical approach as pompous and irrelevant to our time. I hope music will become music again as it has been for centuries from Palestrina to Fauré, Ravel and Debussy.' ~ We toasted each other's health in a last glass of sherry and I departed, with profound sadness and yet elation. The old man waved from the window until my car had disappeared from sight.

THE RT. HON. WINSTON LEONARD SPENCER CHURCHILL, P.C., C.H.

Prime Minister of England 1940-5 and 1951-5, historian and artist. Born 1874; descendant of the Duke of Marlborough; son of Lord Randolph Churchill; his mother, Jennie Jerome, was American. Educated at Harrow and Sandhurst. Went into the Army in 1895, served in Boer War and in World War I. Entered Parliament in 1900 as Conservative; belonged to Liberal party, 1906-24, then rejoined Conservatives. Member of the House from 1900 and holder of many ministerial posts. Fiercely opposed Conservative Prime Minister Neville Chamberlain's policy of appeasement towards Nazi Germany.

As a private citizen I approached Winston Churchill in 1941 with awe. He was more than the Great Man of the twentieth century; he was even more than an institution. He has become, and will always remain, a gigantic passage in human history. But as a photographer I had a job to be done and it must be done far too fast. ~ Mr. Churchill, as he was then, had been addressing the Canadian Parliament in Ottawa on December 30; he was in no mood for portraiture and two minutes were all he would allow me as he passed from the House of Commons Chamber to an ante-room—two niggardly minutes in which I must try to put on film a man who had already written or inspired a library of books, baffled all his biographers, filled the world with his fame, and me, on this occasion, with dread. ~ He marched in scowling, and regarded my camera as he might regard the German enemy. His expression suited me perfectly, if I could capture it, but the cigar thrust between his teeth seemed somehow incompatible with such a solemn and formal occasion. Instinctively I removed the cigar. At this the Churchillian scowl deepened, the head was thrust forward belligerently, and the hand placed on the hip in an attitude of anger. So he stands in my portrait in what has always seemed to me the image of England in those years, defiant and unconquerable. ~ With a swift change of mood, he came towards me when I was finished, extending his hand and saying, 'Well, you can certainly make a roaring lion stand still to be photographed.'

THE RT. HON. SIR WINSTON LEONARD SPENCER CHURCHILL, K.G., P.C., O.M., C.H.

Fifteen years after the portrait on the preceding page was made, I flew the Atlantic to photograph Sir Winston again. This time, I was told, the job would be still more difficult. In fact, it might well be impossible. I was warned that 'the old man must not be tired. You musn't press him. Besides, he's unpredictable. Be quick ... don't make him impatient. Remember, only one or two exposures.' ~ I awaited him at the Drapers' Hall in the City of London, and as he appeared on the stairway I saw how greatly he had changed since our meeting in Ottawa. The massive strength was still there but it had slowed down. The man of action had become a man of thought. Yet what thoughts moved behind that magnificent and battered face only Sir Winston knew. ~ I had not time for much speculation. Only a few minutes could be spared for a photograph. His frown, more alarming than ever, made me fear the worst. To my amazement, he allowed me to lead him to a chair and settled into it after only a few friendly grunts of protest. He looked into the camera with the air of a kindly, innocent old uncle who is a little hard of hearing and finds his chair uncomfortable. ~ I studied that incredible man for a moment and saw a face lined with wisdom and experience, eyes that observed the world with patience, knowledge, authority, and no illusions; and behind this familiar visage I detected an impish, never failing sense of humour without which, I suppose, he could not have survived his long ordeal. ~ Here was England incarnate. I was watching, it seemed to me, old John of Gaunt himself and in the background 'this other Eden, demi-Paradise.' At this sudden flash of communication I clicked the shutter to record a Churchill aged, tired, but immortal.

RENÉ CLAIR

French author and film producer. Born René Chomette, 1898. Started career as a journalist and writer; since 1930's one of Europe's leading film producers; has also worked in English film studios and in Hollywood. His films include: The Italian Straw Hat, Sous les toits de Paris, A nous la liberté, And Then There Were None, Les Belles-de-nuit, Les Grandes Manœuvres, Le Million, *and* Porte des lilas.

Though he has given the world some of its greatest cinematic productions, René Clair is the least dramatic and certainly one of the most modest men I have ever photographed. He sat for me in his Paris home in 1954. He moves about lightly, like a ballerina. He speaks softly. But in everything he says about his work and the work of others there is a fire of conviction. He is a clear-headed, self-contained man who knows his own mind and has mastered his own art. ∼ His opinions of the motion picture world, although always expressed with humility, are clear and decisive. Thus he told me, when I pressed him, that he thought Gina Lollobrigida the greatest actress on the screen at the moment. No, he was not thinking of her superbly statuesque figure (I believe him) but of her real talent as an artist. She was equally brilliant, he said, in comedy and tragedy, even if the public eye might be distracted from that fact by her physical beauty. ∼ As to the screen, he told me that he was not at all in favour of Cinemascope. 'If any change in the size of the screen had to occur,' he remarked, 'I would have much preferred that it be vertical rather than horizontal.' Having expressed this opinion, Clair did not argue it. He does not need to argue in conversation. His arguments, usually irrefutable, appear visually on the screen. Such an attitude is surely appropriate to one who works with film. For even now M. Clair's words, written in the twenties in connection with silent films, can be usefully recalled. 'A fragment of film becomes "pure cinema" as soon as a sensation is aroused through purely visual means... at the present stage, the main task of a film director is to smuggle the greatest possible amount of purely visual themes into a scenario designed to please everybody. Consequently, the literary quality of a scenario has no importance.' 'The only poetry that can exist in a film is the poetry created by the shot itself.' ∼ At the conclusion of the sitting Clair's son joined us. He is an able fashion magazine photographer and his father showed me some of his work. I sensed that Clair was prouder of his son's achievements than of his own. ∼ It was refreshing and exceedingly rare to meet such genuine modesty, especially in a man of such notable success in the film world, a world not notable for that particular quality. Perhaps this modesty springs from his realization that 'in film-making, what survives is not the film, but the inspiration that film can become for future film-makers. The shades gliding across the screen are swallowed into their own dark kingdom even more rapidly than the bodies they reflected. Flickering for a moment in the light of the magic lantern they vanish like moths into the night.'

PAUL CLAUDEL

French poet, playwright, and diplomatist (1868-1955). Held many diplomatic appointments: Ambassador to Japan, 1921-6, to the United States, 1927-33, and to Belgium, 1933-5. A great mystic poet and one of the most important Catholicists of his day. His publications include: L'Otage, Partage de midi (a play), La Jeune Fille Violaine and Poèmes de guerre. At one time the composer Darius Milhaud was his secretary and set many of his poems to music, notably Le Livre de Christophe Colomb.

The French diplomat who had turned playwright and then mystic received me, in 1954, as a great gentleman of the old school at his Château de Brangues in the Isère. He seemed to be a perfect portrait of courtesy and charm. For all his eighty-six years he stood erect, but I noticed that he moved with studied deliberation as if conserving his energies and I quickly discovered that his hearing was much impaired. ∼ We worked in the setting of his library. It would be best, I realized, not to ask too many questions but to let Claudel talk, or not, as he desired. Being himself highly sensitive, he must have understood my feelings immediately. He therefore took charge of the conversation without any prompting from me. ∼ He talked, with a gaiety which could not quite hide the tragic memories, about the German wartime occupation of his *château*. The Nazis had allowed him to keep a few rooms for his own use and he had got along quite well, he said, especially after his wife had devised more than twenty ways of cooking turnips, the only food available, since the invaders disliked this vegetable. Claudel recalled that experience without bitterness. He evidently had no time for recrimination. ∼ As it happened, he had just returned that day from Paris where he had seen Ingrid Bergman's performance in his *Jeanne d'Arc au bûcher*. Yes, he said, it had been an interesting performance but quite different from any other actress's interpretation of his work. I was not sure that he approved of Miss Bergman's version, but French gallantry would not have permitted him to say more. ∼ Then, as I was a Canadian, he turned the conversation to my country and recalled that while serving as French Ambassador to Washington he had there become a friend of Mr. Vincent Massey, now Governor-General of Canada. It may be news to most Canadians that Mr. Massey once played the part of 'A Pope' in Claudel's play *The Hostage*, produced privately by certain eminent amateurs of the stage. 'And,' said Claudel, 'Mr. Massey played the part very well indeed.' ∼ When I prepared to leave, he accompanied me to my car and bade me a warm farewell. On hearing of his death not long afterwards I remembered him thus, an erect and splendid figure at the doorway of his *château*, where even the Nazis could not long disturb his serenity.

JEAN COCTEAU

French poet, novelist, playwright, critic, and film producer. Born 1889. His first volume of poems, La Lampe d'Aladin, was published when he was seventeen and was followed shortly after by two more. Cocteau later 'disowned' these publications; he dates his literary début from his prose fantasy Le Potomak, 1917. Since then he has experimented with all means of expression including the ballet, the circus, and jazz. A few of his best known works are: La Machine infernale (play), L'Aigle a deux têtes (play), La Belle et la Bête (film), Orphée (film), Les Enfants terribles (novel and film). Member of the Académie Française, Officier Légion d'Honneur.

Time did not permit me, in 1949, to photograph M. Cocteau in his beautiful country home and he, of course, was busy with a thousand things . . . this master-of-all-arts and insatiable experimenter with life. We arranged, therefore, to take the pictures in a friend's apartment, directly above Cocteau's tiny Paris office. ~ As a stage and film director, and in later years a painter, he understood at once what I was trying to do. He looked on with interest as the lighting was prepared and backgrounds chosen, but, an old 'pro' himself, he did not attempt to direct me and I was pleased to have his confidence. ~ He chatted freely about many things, his thoughts bubbling over, and his face, infinitely expressive, altering momentarily with his mood. ~ He had definite ideas on the theatre, the film, and the written word, with all of which he has been brilliantly successful. 'Of course,' he said, 'there are subjects more suitable for the film than for the stage, especially where many scenes and changes of locale must be made. Other stories, perfect for the stage, would be lost on film. But again, there are many stories that are best left alone by both film and stage. They must be written.' ~ When I asked him whom he considered the greatest living actor and actress, M. Cocteau was non-committal. But he warmly defended the current generation of the stage. 'I think,' he remarked, 'that there are many more good actors and actresses now than at any time in the past. Why, if some of the great actors or actresses of older days were to come back now they would find that they were far from achieving the high standard attained by many of their successors today.' ~ How did he view the attempts of many governments the world over to take a hand in artistic productions? 'The state,' he insisted, 'should subsidize the arts as is done in France—the Comédie Française, and Les Beaux Arts, for example. But the state must never dictate to them. A creative artist must not be restricted. He must be free to express himself without any hindrance whatsoever.' ~ As I was leaving, Cocteau bemoaned the fact that most actors did not know to use their hands naturally, clumsy use had become 'some sort of occupational disease.' Cocteau himself was thoroughly immune: his hands are as eloquent, dramatic, and sensitive as his face. And this man's whole being, physical, mental, and spiritual, is poured into his work with reckless prodigality.

AARON COPLAND

American composer. Born 1900; studied at Fontainebleau School of Music, 1921, and with Mme Nadia Boulanger in Paris, 1921-4. Returned to United States, 1924; held Guggenheim Fellowship, 1925-7; Lecturer in Music, New School for Social Research, New York, 1927-37; organized Copland-Sessions Concerts with Roger Sessions, 1928-31; founder, American Festivals of Contemporary Music, Yaddo, Saratoga Springs, N.Y., 1932; taught composition at Harvard University, 1935-44, and at Berkshire Music Center, of which he is now Assistant Director, 1940; toured South America, 1941 and 1947; Charles Eliot Norton Professor of Poetry, Harvard, 1951-2. Director, League of Composers, Edward MacDowell Association, Koussevitsky Music Foundation, etc. Works include the ballets Billy the Kid, Appalachian Spring *(which won the New York Music Critics Circle Award, 1945), and* Rodeo, *settings for* Twelve Poems *by Emily Dickinson, various works for orchestra and for solo instruments, and film scores. Awarded Pulitzer Prize, 1944, and an award from the Academy of Motion Picture Arts and Sciences for the film score of* The Heiress, *1950.*

Arriving at Ossining, New York, on a chilly spring morning in 1956, I saw on a hilltop a gracious and rambling house which commanded a fine view of the country for miles around. Aaron Copland was absent from his home at the moment. His secretary explained that he had been called away on an urgent matter but would return in a few minutes. Meanwhile, a huge fire was lit in the library and I was entertained, after my cold ride, with excellent coffee. ∼ The atmosphere of that house was friendly and informal. It had once been a combination barn and carriage house, I was told, and I marvelled at the skilful remodelling which had transformed it. Immediately I began to enjoy myself, not a usual sensation when one is about to photograph a complete stranger. Presently the master of the house appeared, and there was about him a certain candour and friendliness that endeared him to me at once. ∼ As we began to talk casually about books and about his own music and that of other composers, I soon found Mr. Copland had a keen critical sense, though always a friendly one. We talked about some of our favourite musicians whom I had photographed and he referred with affection to his great teacher, Nadia Boulanger, expressing the hope that I would also photograph her some day. ∼ Like himself, Mr. Copland's writings about music, as I later discovered, have an ease and charm which make even the most abstruse musical question accessible and interesting to a layman. Indeed, the problem of communication between composer and listener has greatly concerned him and on it he has made a number of wise observations. He has warned composers that 'isolation breeds an ingrown quality, an overrefinement, a too great complexity both of technique and of sentiment. The composer who is frightened at losing his artistic integrity through contact with a mass audience is no longer aware of the meaning of the word art.' He has also reminded listeners that 'music can only be really alive when there are listeners who are really alive. To listen intently, to listen consciously, to listen with one's whole intelligence is the least we can do in the furtherance of an art that is one of the glories of mankind,' for 'the artist should feel himself affirmed and buoyed up by his community. In other words, art and the life of art must mean something, in the deepest sense, to the everyday citizen. When that happens, America will have achieved a maturity to which every sincere artist will have contributed.'

KATHARINE CORNELL

American actress-manager. Born of American parents in Berlin, 1898. Made her stage début with the Washington Square Players in New York, 1916, and has been especially successful in several plays by Bernard Shaw, and in The Barretts of Wimpole Street. *Plays in which Miss Cornell has appeared recently are* The Constant Wife *(1951-2),* The Prescott Proposals *(1953-4), and* The Dark is Light Enough *(1954-5). She married Guthrie McClintic, theatrical producer and director, in 1921; he has directed many of the plays in which she has starred.*

The finely chiselled face and delicate genius of Katharine Cornell had fascinated me long before I saw them at close range. The voice, which I had heard so often in the theatre, seemed to me as intriguing as the face and was the final expression of the genius. When I was invited to tea at Miss Cornell's New York house in 1947, I found her sensitive, quick-witted, and filled with a salty sort of humour. Here was a great actress playing her greatest part—herself. ∼ She had been glancing over some letters from George Bernard Shaw for whom she had earned a million dollars or so by acting in his *Candida*, and she read snatches of this inimitable correspondence with hoots of laughter. Because their distant partnership of the theatre had been so profitable, G.B.S. referred to her in these letters as 'My Million Dollar Baby'—a queer title for the queen of the American stage, but Miss Cornell seemed to appreciate it. ∼ I asked her whom she considered to be among the great women of America. Her reply was quick and decisive, 'Helen Keller and Martha Graham—and happily they are friends of mine. I would like you to photograph them.' (This I did later on.) And Miss Cornell began to talk about Helen Keller, whom she deeply admired. ∼ The conversation was very pleasant but I had not yet found a way of representing the actress against her proper background, the stage. Finally I asked her to wear one of the numerous scarves which had been presented to her. Instantly grasping my intent, she seemed, for a moment, to be performing one of her famous roles. Yet when my camera actually caught her, she was being herself, and this too was what I wanted.

ALFRED CORTOT

Swiss pianist, composer, and conductor. Born 1877; studied at the Paris Conservatoire. In 1902 Richard Wagner's widow entrusted him with the direction of Götterdämmerung and Tristan und Isolde. One-time Professor at the Paris Conservatoire and Conductor of the Paris Symphony Orchestra. Founder of the musical trio of Cortot, Casals, and Thibaud (violinist). Has made many concert tours abroad and three volumes of his piano music have been published. At present Director of the Ecole Normale de Musique, Paris, and lives in Lausanne, Switzerland.

The Ecole Normale de Musique in Paris is a rather imposing structure on the outside. The inside was much the worse for wear when I saw it in 1954. It seemed to me that one might almost say the exact opposite of the school's founder. Despite his age, Alfred Cortot's heart is young. ∼ It was difficult in his venerable institution to find a suitable background for my portrait. Eventually I decided on the 'Salle Cortot,' the master's special corner in the school where he continues to teach and of which he remains the moving spirit, dividing his time between Paris and his home in Lausanne. ∼ Naturally, I mentioned to him that I was going to photograph his old friend, Pablo Casals, in a few days, for I knew that Casals, Cortot, and Thibaud were the original members of a most famous musical trio. M. Cortot spoke lovingly of Casals, asked me to take him warm greetings, and added: 'Strange as it may appear, the trio never had "words" during the whole of our association.' I could well believe that so far as Cortot was concerned —a benign and gentle soul, idolized by his staff, and still, in his old age, an incurable romantic. ∼ I asked him if he thought there would ever be a trio as great as his partnership with Casals and Thibaud. He smiled: 'It would hardly be my place, would it, to say "No." But I feel nowadays that the younger generation is not quite as willing as we old-timers were to play as members of a group. They all want recognition individually.' Cortot, I could see, was long past this sort of vanity if, indeed, he had ever felt it.

CECIL B. DE MILLE

American film director. Born in 1881 in Ashfield, Massachusetts; died 1959; identified with motion pictures since 1913. Previously a playwright and theatrical producer. President of Cecil B. de Mille Productions Inc. until 1951; Director, Paramount Pictures Corporation. Recent productions include Samson and Delilah, The Greatest Show on Earth, *and* The Ten Commandments. *In 1949 received special Award from the Academy of Motion Picture Arts and Sciences for '35 years of pioneering in motion pictures.'*

If the great motion picture director knew how to give directions, he also knew how to take them. When I photographed him in 1956 both at his home and at his studio, and made sharp demands on his time and patience, he gave no sign of temperament. No actor could have been more co-operative and understanding than the man who has directed, tamed, and made so many actors. ~ Though no longer young, Mr. de Mille had the energy, bounce, and animation of a youthful beginner in Hollywood. When I asked him if he had considered retirement, he retorted: 'I'll take pictures as long as I'm allowed to.' ~ Did he think that all pictures, biblical ones especially, should carry a message? 'Not necessarily so, but if it is possible to give the world a message by this method you may be failing in your responsibility when you do not. On the other hand, it would be fatal if everything was slanted in this way, especially for entertainment purposes.' ~ I asked him how stage actors fitted into the needs of the movies. 'The face,' he said, 'is the greatest canvas you can paint on. Actors who have played on the stage and then come in front of the camera present a problem. Their eyes are used to distances of a hundred feet or more and so they use them artificially. But no one can fool the camera. Anything synthetic shows up immediately. If the actor's eyes are not telling the truth, the camera finds him out. It is only when he has learned to use his eyes naturally that close-ups can be safely made. Why, Yul Brynner's eyes go to depths that no one has fully probed.' ~ As I was asking Mr. de Mille constantly to change his attitude and expression, he looked up at me suddenly and exclaimed: 'You're like David Wark Griffith. He was the first man who could photograph thought and you can—and do.' Then he added: 'Afterwards, Griffith taught us all how to do it.' ~ Naturally there was much talk between us about de Mille's *Ten Commandments*, then in production, and at one point a rather meticulous public relations man asked whether it was proper to rest the manuscript of this picture, as well as the subject's hand, on the Bible. To which de Mille replied with spirit: 'I know nothing better for my hands to rest on—do you?'

CHRISTIAN DIOR

French couturier (1905-1957). Educated at the Lycée Gerson, and the Ecole des Sciences Politiques, Paris. Set up an art gallery to exhibit works of little known artists. In 1935 entered world of fashion designing and shortly after the newspaper Figaro asked for his designs. Served in French Army, 1939-40, and after the Nazi occupation lived in the south of France, 1940-2. Worked for Lucien Lelong in his fashion house, 1942-6; in 1947 opened his own establishment in Paris. Dior's 'New Look' revolutionized post-war fashions and became a household word throughout Europe and the United States.

Perhaps the most successful, certainly the most suave and disarming, dictator of our time was a man with a gentle, oval-shaped face, pensive eyes, and an elongated nose. Christian Dior held more elegant women in abject slavery than any pasha, but he shunned publicity and was surrounded by secretaries and functionaries whose only task was to keep away photographers and journalists. ∼ Clearly I had come to Paris at the wrong time in 1954, within a few days of a Dior opening, when the contents of the salon were more carefully guarded than any secret of state. Any premature inkling of the master's latest creations, I gathered, would create an international crisis. Hence the only place where Dior would be photographed was his tiny private office which guards the designing and model room. His press attaché understood my problem, but nothing could be done: 'Anywhere else there would be gowns in course of preparation or models being fitted with new creations, or sketches, or. . . .' I understood. No room except the office could be visited even to get a more suitable chair, table, or prop of any kind. Dior could perhaps be portrayed with some sketches of gowns, but, of course, they would be gowns of previous years. And I was reminded that my subject had little time to devote to his own portrait when, as he has said, he was so desperately trying to improve the look of womankind and 'save it from nature.' This task was so demanding, indeed, that he seldom left his office day or night and at this critical season his food was brought to his desk. There I was compelled, against my wishes, to make his portrait, and to arrange lights and camera in such a space was something of a feat. When Dior appeared at last I was amazed at the contrast between the man and the feverish, conspiratorial air maintained around him. The arbiter of style, who has made skirts long or short, busts grow or fade by a flick of his pencil, was himself dressed in a very quiet business suit. Though thoroughly French, he looked exactly like the personification of an English understatement. His manner was charming, if somewhat preoccupied, and he understood, as an artist, that I wished to make a fine portrait of him. Alas, the time element. . . . ∼ I decided to portray him in his authentic element of mystery. I therefore placed him standing partially hidden behind a screen, only a portion of the face showing, with just one eye lighted and his finger to his lips enjoining silence and secrecy.

WALT DISNEY

Artist and producer of animated sound cartoons; Chairman of Walt Disney Productions Ltd. since 1928. Born in Chicago, 1901. 'Father' of Mickey Mouse, Donald Duck, and many other now universally beloved cartoon characters. Some of his best known films are Three Little Pigs, Snow White and the Seven Dwarfs, Fantasia, *and* Pinocchio. *Recently has been concentrating on real-life nature films such as* The Living Desert, The Vanishing Prairie, *and* The African Lion; *made* Davy Crockett *into a children's hero throughout much of the world. Holds many awards and citations.*

'Who do you think I am—Captain Nemo?' said Walt Disney when I came to photograph him in Hollywood in 1956, for the second time. Yes, I did think that Nemo, the name of the gallant captain in *Twenty Thousand Leagues under the Sea*, was exactly the right name for Disney because, of course, it means nobody. And nobody else on earth is like Disney who is quite unlike his works. ～ To prepare myself I asked some members of Disney's swarming entourage what subject of conversation would interest him and reveal something of the inner man. Everyone's answer was the same: 'Talk to him about Disneyland. It's his most cherished project.' I therefore journeyed one Sunday morning to Disneyland and inspected with amazement the world of wonders created by the imagination of one mind. Clearly this might be a setting for Disney's portrait, a setting of pure fantasy. ～ We took some shots against a background of the entrance to a mammoth underground cave which had been used in *Twenty Thousand Leagues under the Sea* (although for the portrait opposite a background more familiar to his audiences was chosen). Disney sat down in front of the cave entrance, nonchalant, relaxed, and genial as he always appears with strangers, his boyish manner hiding what his associates told me was the fierce drive of the perfectionist. I gave him a copy of the *Disneyland News* to look at and, eyeing me impishly, he solemnly read out: 'Disneyland is being sued for two and a half million dollars.' When I offered him a cigarette he refused it. He never allows himself to be photographed while smoking, or with a drink. He has his large audience of children the world over to think of. ～ I asked him particularly about his children's motion pictures, such as *Snow White*, and found him eager to discuss them. He intended, he said, to return more and more to the use of animation in place of living actors. Already he had filled many filing cabinets with drawings for one of his next ventures. ～ All this, I suggested, was far removed from the realities in documentary pictures such as *The Living Desert* where cruelty in nature is revealed so starkly. 'Nature,' said Disney, 'is concerned with the survival of the fittest. She is unlike man who kills for the sake of killing.' Under the breezy surface this man evidently had thought a good deal about grimness. But then, only a very serious man can provide the sense of fantasy which, in the guise of pleasant madness, helps the world to keep its sanity.

H.R.H. THE PRINCE PHILIP, DUKE OF EDINBURGH

PRINCE OF THE UNITED KINGDOM OF GREAT BRITAIN
AND NORTHERN IRELAND, EARL OF MERIONETH,
BARON GREENWICH OF GREENWICH IN THE
COUNTY OF LONDON, K.G., K.T.

ALBERT EINSTEIN

Physicist; discoverer and exponent of the theory of relativity. Born in Switzerland in 1879 and died in the United States in 1955. After holding appointments at the Universities of Zürich and Prague, he was appointed Professor of Physics at Berlin University and Director of the Kaiser Wilhelm Institute for Physics in 1914; he became a German citizen. He renounced this citizenship and his appointment in 1933, left Europe for the United States, and was made a member for life of the Institute for Advanced Study at Princeton. In 1940 he became an American citizen. During World War II he did research work on explosives for the United States Navy.

Among the tasks that life as a photographer had set me, a portrait of Albert Einstein had always seemed a 'must'—not only because this greatest refugee of our century has been accounted by all the world (except his homeland) as the outstanding scientist since Newton, but because his face, in all its rough grandeur, invited and challenged the camera. ∼ When I saw him for the first time at Princeton University's Institute for Advanced Study, in February 1948, I found exactly what I had expected—a simple, kindly, almost childlike man, too great for any of the tricks or postures of eminence. Yet one did not have to understand his science to feel at once the power of his mind. ∼ Awed before this unique intellect, I yet ventured to ask Einstein his views on human immortality. He mused for a moment and then replied: 'What I believe of immortality? There are two kinds. The first lives in the imagination of people and is thus an illusion. There is a relative immortality which may conserve the memory of an individual for some generations. But there is only one true immortality, on a cosmic scale, and that is the immortality of the cosmos itself. There is no other.' ∼ He spoke of these ultimate mysteries as calmly as he might answer a student's question about mathematics—with such an air of quiet confidence, indeed, that I found his answer profoundly disturbing to one who held other views. I turned the conversation, and knowing him to be an accomplished violinist, asked if there were any connection between music and mathematics. 'In art,' he said, 'and in the higher ranges of science, there is a feeling of harmony which underlies all endeavour. There is no true greatness in art or science without that sense of harmony. He who lacks it can never be more than a great technician in either field.' ∼ Was he optimistic about the future harmony of mankind itself? He appeared to ponder deeply and remarked in graver tones: 'Optimistic? No. But if mankind fails to find a harmonious solution then there will be disaster on a dimension beyond anyone's imagination.' To what source should we look for the hope of the world's future? 'To ourselves,' said Einstein. ∼ He spoke sadly yet serenely, as one who had looked into the universe far past mankind's small affairs. In this humour my camera caught him . . . the portrait of a man beyond hope or despair.

DWIGHT D. EISENHOWER

President of the United States 1953-. Born in Denison, Texas, 1890; graduated from the United States Military Academy, West Point, in 1915. Commissioned as Second Lieutenant in the Infantry of the United States Army in 1915 and advanced through the grades until appointed General of the Army in December 1944. Supreme Commander, Expeditionary Forces, Allied Armies in the re-conquest of Western Europe from Nazi Germany; Chief of Staff of United States Army, 1945-8. President of Columbia University, 1948-52. First Supreme Commander of North Atlantic Treaty Forces (NATO) in Europe 1950-2. Holds numerous decorations. Retired from the army in 1952 to become Republican presidential candidate.

I photographed Dwight Eisenhower first in 1946 when he was known only as a great soldier, and I have naturally followed with intense interest his adventure into politics. ∼ After he had given his maiden speech as a contender for the Republican nomination, I found myself at a small gathering of editors and political writers in Ottawa. These men seemed to agree that Mr. Eisenhower could not beat Senator Taft. Only because I had made a portrait of the General, and not because I knew much of politics, these experts asked me what I thought of his chances. I took a deep breath and replied, 'Not only will Eisenhower win from Taft, but he will win on the first ballot.' Of course I was called naïve by the experts and one of them proposed that I back my judgment with a modest wager of ten dollars. When the result was known, I received a letter from this gentleman: 'My dear Karsh, you are as good a political prophet as you are a photographer. Here are my ten bucks.' Promptly I returned the cheque and kept the letter as a souvenir. ∼ Shortly afterwards I arranged to make a new portrait of Eisenhower, this time in the middle of the necessities of the 1952 presidential campaign. His mood that day was all wrong for my purpose. As the soldier he had seemed relaxed, confident, imperturbable. The portrait opposite shows a calm face and a clear eye reflecting a man certain of his course. Now I found him restless, worried, and, I suspected, uncertain. How could I provoke the right mood for my camera? Then I thought of my bet. Happily the letter from the editor was in my pocket; so I showed it to Mr. Eisenhower and asked him to autograph it. The absurd little incident seemed to divert him. He relaxed completely and revealed that happy disposition which makes everybody 'like Ike.' ∼ I had long known, however, that behind the boyish smile there was a strong faith and a profound trust in mankind, and yet the pain of a man who has watched tragedy at first hand. After this, my first portrait, I had sent him a copy of the book in which it appeared initially. He wrote me at some length, of his 'belief that through universal understanding and knowledge there is some hope that order and logic can gradually replace chaos and hysteria in the world. It occurs to me that in publishing this book you may have contributed in some definite way towards helping the peoples of the world to a better understanding of each other.' I hope that may be true in some fashion of both books. ∼ When Mr. Eisenhower became President I framed the letter he had autographed and sent it to the editor who had lost the bet, saying: 'The story is now complete.' But at that time the story of Eisenhower, the statesman, was just beginning.

ELIZABETH THE SECOND

BY THE GRACE OF GOD, OF THE UNITED KINGDOM
OF GREAT BRITAIN AND NORTHERN IRELAND
AND OF HER OTHER REALMS AND TERRITORIES,
QUEEN, HEAD OF THE COMMONWEALTH,
DEFENDER OF THE FAITH

GEORGES ENESCO

Rumanian composer. Born in 1881 and died in Paris in 1955. When aged seven he was studying in Vienna and composing sonatas, rondos, and various other works. Later he was admitted to the Paris Conservatoire where he studied violin and composition; at seventeen he made his début as a composer with 'Poème Roumain.' He was also a conductor, pianist, and violinist. Evolved a personal style based largely on Rumanian folk tunes. Works include orchestral and chamber music, also an opera, Oedipus. Was principal teacher of Yehudi Menuhin whose talent he was the first to recognize.

The apartment of Georges Enesco in Paris was less than modest. It was poverty itself. Yet it contained certain riches and an extraordinary musician who sat amid a clutter of relics and mementos recalling for him, no doubt, the happier days of the past. ∼ I knew that he had a serious heart condition, but I also found that he was so badly crippled by arthritis that he moved as little as possible. His desk was placed so that he could turn from it to his piano without rising from his chair. He looked frail, old, and exhausted, but at times I caught in his eyes a sparkle which seemed to illuminate his whole face with intense kindliness and unshakable courage. ∼ At this moment, in 1954, he was putting the final touches to an orchestral work, now almost ready for the publishers. I was amazed at the neatness of his musical script, written meticulously in ink. ∼ I did not like to disturb his creative thought, I knew that this photographic sitting must tire him, and I hesitated to ask many questions. But I could not refrain from inquiring his opinion of the music of modern composers. 'Some of it I like,' he said, 'but a great deal I do not. I know less of Britten's work than of the others. I like some of Stravinsky's, especially part of his *Firebird*. Also some of Khachaturyan whom I consider the most normal of modern composers . . . normal in the sense that his music is derived from folklore and is nearer than most to the classical ideas of music.' Whom did he regard as the greatest living conductor? 'Furtwängler, without a doubt. Bruno Walter is great also and, at times, Mitropolous who, I think, has a fantastic brain capacity.' ∼ Remembering that I had heard Enesco play the violin years earlier, I wanted to know if modern violins compared with those of Stradivarius or the Amati? He replied with a twinkle: 'Let me tell you a little story. When I used to play the violin long ago I was often criticized because there did not seem to be enough strength and force to my playing. One day the French *luthier*, Kaul, said he would make a violin for me. I insisted that I must pay for it. Very well, said Kaul, two thousand francs. The violin was made and after that when I played it all the critics remarked on the depth, strength, and beauty of my playing!' ∼ Enesco obviously was tired and busy, but in his old age he had not lost his interest in youth. After the sitting he intended to give an audition to a nine-year-old violinist who had come all the way from Italy to seek the master's advice. Such young aspirants, said Enesco, must be encouraged for 'who knows but that some day we may discover another Menuhin!' ∼ As I prepared to leave, Enesco turned to his piano and announced that he would treat me to something light and gay. Then, with the knuckles of his crippled hands, he played a charming little Chinese tune. It still haunts my memory whenever I think of that indomitable old man who lived, almost literally I think, on the nourishment of music.

SIR JACOB EPSTEIN, K.B.E.

Sculptor. Born in 1880 in New York of Russian-Polish parents; settled in London in 1905 and is now a British subject. Works include: the tomb of Oscar Wilde in Paris; 'Rima' memorial to W. H. Hudson in Hyde Park; 'Venus'; 'Christ'; 'The Visitation' and 'The Madonna and Child' in London's Tate Gallery; busts of Lord Beaverbrook, Chaim Weizman, Albert Einstein, and George Bernard Shaw. Has created many controversial pieces of modern sculpture.

When I entered Sir Jacob Epstein's London home in 1943, he came down the stairs, greeted me warmly, observed the two Canadian soldiers who served as my assistants that day, looked at my equipment, and then burst into tears. Without a word he rushed back up the stairs. ∼ As the years passed the tears remained an unsolved mystery, but I was determined that some day I would photograph Epstein. Alas, after all the necessary arrangements had been made for a second try, I found the great sculptor suffering from an eye infection. ∼ There was no sign of temperament on this day. Epstein graciously showed me about a studio filled with his massive and awe-inspiring work. I was especially attracted by a metal sketch-model of a Madonna and Child, and resolved to photograph it for use on our personal Christmas card, if he would let me. He was loath to part with it, even for a few hours, but finally agreed to send it to my hotel. It arrived, meticulously wrapped in cotton-batting, with minute recommendations for its care. My wife, too, fell immediately under the spell of this statue; in the end we acquired it for our home in Ottawa and returned happy . . . but without a portrait. ∼ My third try, in 1955, was a complete success. To leave this restless man free for movement I decided to use electronic flash lights. He walked about his studio, talking all the time and apparently unconscious of my camera. It was only when I developed my films that I realized an odd coincidence. His hand had adopted the attitude of the hand in the monumental sculpture which I had used as a background. I suspected then that he must have used his own hand as a model. ∼ In the middle of a tiring afternoon, he suggested a break for tea. I agreed a rest might give us additional inspiration. 'Inspiration?' he retorted, 'I never lack inspiration.' A bold assumption, but the jungle of statuary around us confirmed it. ∼ After tea he took me to a little room where, in a glass enclosure, he had placed some of his treasures. My eye fell at once upon a sculpture of two birds in white marble and I felt that it belonged in our home, which, being inveterate bird-watchers, we call 'Little Wings.' Epstein would not sell his marble birds, but he did then and there design a base for this sculpture, which I saw as the centre of a fountain. He sat down again at the tea table and began drawing a sketch. 'This,' he said, 'is how I see it.' Of course, he had seen it perfectly. Now, whenever I walk about our grounds, I visualize the fountain, capped by those lovely birds, glistening in a spray of water—a fragment of his vision of beauty.

DAME EDITH EVANS, D.B.E.

British actress. Début in London, 1912, when she played Cressida in Troilus and Cressida. *Has appeared in many plays mainly in London's West End but also on Broadway. The latest plays in which she has acted include* Waters of the Moon *(1951-3),* The Dark Is Light Enough *(1954), and* The Chalk Garden *(1956-7); starred in the films* The Queen of Spades *and* The Importance of Being Earnest.

Christopher Fry's play *The Dark Is Light Enough* was, in 1954, new on the London stage and, like all his work, it impressed me deeply. But as a photographer I was even more excited by the performance of Dame Edith Evans in the leading role. Here, I saw at once, was an artist whose portrait simply must be added to my collection. Immediately after the performance I telephoned Fry and expressed my desire to make this portrait. He agreed that Dame Edith was one of the great people of the stage and assuredly deserved a place in any gallery of contemporary genius. There would be no difficulty about it, said Fry. He would arrange everything. So he did, like the kindly, competent man he is—as well as a playwright of the first magnitude. ~ The arrangements, though by no means perfect, were the best that could be devised in Dame Edith's busy and strictly scheduled life. She would be photographed on the stage some time before the evening performance of Fry's play. ~ It is unwise, as a rule, to photograph an artist just in advance of a performance when a feeling of suspense and nervousness, common to all real artists at these moments, is likely to creep into the portrait despite all the photographer's efforts to avoid it. Thus, if the expression in this picture shows a trace of impatience, even of arrogance, it is quite natural. Dame Edith was thinking entirely, as I knew, of the performance ahead of her. Like all artists she was absorbed in her work and had already begun to transform herself, as it were, into another person, her role in the play. No actress worthy of that title can ever feel at ease until the curtain has risen. ~ But although I was disappointed at first when I could not photograph her in a mood of relaxation, on second thought it seemed to me that the stage, with the atmosphere it acquires before the play begins, might in another way yet be the right setting for an actress after all. ~ When I wished to include her hands she said at once that they were not beautiful or worth photographing. I insisted gently and, with the greatest reluctance, she consented. To me, the eloquence and sensitivity of these hands open yet another window on a majestic talent.

SIR ALEXANDER FLEMING, KT.

British bacteriologist (1881-1955). Educated at Kilmarnock Academy and St. Mary's Hospital Medical School. Professor of Bacteriology at St. Mary's Hospital School and in charge of the Wright-Fleming Institute on Microbiology. Knighted, 1944; shared Nobel Prize in Medicine, 1945. Discovered lysozyme in 1922 and penicillin in 1929. Rector of Edinburgh University, 1951-5. Held honorary degrees from many universities in the United States and Europe.

It is said that Sir Alexander Fleming once witnessed a magnificent accident and had the genius to understand its meaning to mankind. A microscopic shred of mould somehow settled on a culture of staphylococci at a London hospital in 1928. The killing germs withered under the touch of this substance. Fleming noted that fact, isolated the mould, grew it, and gave the world penicillin. ~ Naturally, I approached St. Mary's Hospital, London, in 1954 for my meeting with this man in a spirit of admiration. To the embarrassment of his secretary, the great scientist failed to turn up for his appointment. No reason was given for his absence, but I suspected that he was far from well. In the light of subsequent events, my assumption may have been correct. At any rate, he arrived punctually next day, clasped my hand, and apologized profusely for his previous absence. ~ I found a gentleman of white hair, bulging forehead, and clear-blue eyes, obviously a Scot. What struck me most was that simplicity which I had noticed in so many other men of greatness. For example, his microscope had a lens of the most up-to-date sort but the stand was old-fashioned in the extreme. The modern microscope, as compared to Fleming's, was like a Cadillac beside a Model T Ford. But his suited him and it had penetrated some profound mysteries. ~ As we went about our work together I plied him with some of my favourite questions. Who, I asked, was the 'Man of the Century'? 'Well,' said Sir Alexander, 'Winston will be a competitor. Certainly Lenin also. And of course we must not overlook Gandhi.' ~ Where, I inquired, would medicine make its next advance? 'Cancer,' he replied in his laconic Scottish style. ~ In answer to another of my questions Sir Alexander requested one of his associates to bring in from his laboratory the sealed glass tray containing the original mould of penicillin. Since it is one of the most significant exhibits of our age, and a great symbol of the healing arts, I felt it must form an integral part of Fleming's portrait. ~ He told me that before long he hoped to relinquish his administrative duties and devote himself entirely to research. What was he looking for? Nothing less, I was amazed to hear, than a vaccine which would give 'total immunity to disease.' (The same search would be referred to later, when I came to photograph Dr. Jonas Salk.) ~ 'There's so much left to do,' he mused. 'So many problems, you know. I just want to sit and work.' Alas, that opportunity for him and for humanity was soon to be lost.

DAME MARGOT FONTEYN DE ARIAS, D.B.E.

British ballerina. Born 1919; educated in the United States and China. Joined Sadlers Wells Ballet in 1934. As prima ballerina of the Royal Ballet Company, London, has danced all the principal classical roles as well as leading roles in many modern ballets. Has appeared in Austria, Belgium, Canada, Czechoslovakia, Denmark, France, Germany, Italy, the Netherlands, Norway, Poland, Sweden, and the United States. C.B.E., 1951; D.B.E., 1956. In 1955 married Roberto Emilio Arias, Panamanian Ambassador to the Court of St. James, 1955-8.

As it was my only chance, I photographed Margot Fonteyn in 1957 while she was rehearsing, in the Brooklyn studios of N.B.C., for the television spectacular *Cinderella*. A leisurely sitting proved impossible. My brief interlude turned out to be something like a ballet dance for the sedentary photographer! Nevertheless, this remarkable woman, flitting on and off the stage, somehow found time to give me, in disjointed but clear, thoughtful sentences, something of life in the ballet. ∼ She had come to this art, she said, through the influence of her mother who, though not a dancer, frequently attended the ballet, taking her daughter with her. It was not easy, however, for any girl, to make a career of the dance. Out of a starting class of children at the Royal Ballet School, Miss Fonteyn told me, probably not more than five would ever succeed in entering the first company. Some of the others, though, would find opportunities elsewhere—in Canada, for instance—or would switch to the stage or the opera. ∼ Did Miss Fonteyn attend the ballet when she was not herself dancing? 'No,' she said emphatically, 'I either want to be in it or away from it. For my own amusement I go to the opera.' ∼ It must be difficult, I ventured, for a ballerina to adjust her physical movements to stages of different sizes. No such adjustment, she replied, was possible since all ballet movements were standard in performance. On a small stage you just had to do the best you could. As a matter of fact, she added, classical ballet roles hardly changed through the years. 'Some time ago,' she recalled, 'I went to Paris to study with Olga Preobrajenskaya for a ballet in which she had created the leading role. After I had danced it for her, the role remained exactly as she had learned it fifty years before, except for a change in a finger and hand position here and there.' Surely, I suggested, a great ballerina would be permitted some improvisation now and then within the prescribed choreography? 'Oh never,' she said. ∼ Miss Fonteyn was greatly interested in modern ballets, based on English themes. 'Some time back,' she said, 'we did a ballet about life in a Glasgow slum. It went very well. But we wouldn't attempt an American western theme such as *Rodeo*. We simply wouldn't understand it in our bones and sinews the way American dancers would. It would be like asking Americans to interpret Glasgow slum life.' ∼ Miss Fonteyn's work is beautiful but it is exacting. She is a genius and also a worker. The 'prima ballerina assoluta' of our times has a good-humoured, sensible English face, jet-black hair, a delightful disposition, and a large fund of common sense. She is, without ostentation, a Dame of the British Empire, but she seemed to me something much more important . . . an artist, and a thoroughbred.

ROBERT FROST

American poet. Born in San Francisco, 1875. Father died when poet was ten and he moved with his mother back to New England, the usual background for his poems. Studied at Dartmouth College and Harvard University. Has worked as bobbin-boy, editor, farmer, teacher of psychology. Trip to England, 1912, marks beginning of his career as a poet; in 1913 A Boy's Will was published in London and hailed by English poets, including Rupert Brooks and Lascelles Abercrombie. Professor of English at Amherst College, 1916-20, 1923-5, 1926-38; 'poet in residence' at the University of Michigan, 1921-3; Emerson Fellow at Harvard University, 1939-41; Resident Consultant in Humanities, Dartmouth College, since 1943. Helped to found the Breadloaf School at Middlebury College, 1920, and returned every summer as a lecturer. Pulitzer Prize winner in 1924, 1931, 1937, 1943. His works include: A Boy's Will, North of Boston, A Witness Tree, Aforesaid.

'Don't make a saint of me,' said Mr. Frost as he faced my camera in 1958. 'I'm a rascal. Why, they call me Scarface Frost from Chicago.' This was my introduction to the crusty, beloved American poet, an old man who does precisely as he pleases. At the time he was sitting in his littered, chaotic studio at Cambridge, Massachusetts. There he works at what he is pleased to call his desk—a dilapidated piece of Ten-Test supported by a piece of string and a battered walking stick. Yet, I thought, out of all this bedlam comes so much beauty. ~ Some of that native, homely American candour for which he is famous began to appear as we went to work. His mind moved suddenly from one subject to another in long leaps. 'Painting, sculpture, and photography,' he commented, 'may be international but poetry is a medium for the nationalists. The thought may be universal, but the expression of it is nationalistic. I have never seen an instance when one of my poems was translated into a foreign language without losing the idiom of the original.' ~ Then he remembered that T. S. Eliot had once asked him what he meant by the expression, 'Good fences make good neighbours.' Although Frost had not invented that phrase (it was a folk-saying from New England), he was not surprised that Eliot should object to it. 'Eliot's characters,' Mr. Frost said, 'never know boundaries, not even of each other's beds.' ~ He recalled his recent visit to the United Nations in New York, where he had been taken to the Meditation Room. The only symbol there was of pure iron—a symbol of man's strength and unity. At this Frost scoffed and instantly composed a new, derisive couplet to decorate the shrine. He recited it to me: 'Nature within her inmost self divides To trouble men with having to take sides.' ~ 'Those silly people down there,' he said, 'talking about love all the time! They make me hate. You only value one when it's offset by the other. You always have victory and defeat, good and evil, love and hate, God and the devil.' ~ I asked him about his way of writing a poem. He said it was like making a witticism... it just came. 'And,' he added, 'it only comes fifteen or twenty times a year.' ~ Mr. Frost talked at length about his lectures, explaining that he would rather make a speech than read his poetry; every poem says all he has to say on that subject. When I told him that I would come to his next lecture in order to ask him questions, he said, 'Hmph, you will be the only one that does.'

CHRISTOPHER FRY

British dramatist; born 1907. Taught at Hazelwood Preparatory School 1928-31. Director, Tunbridge Wells Repertory Players, 1932-5; Oxford Repertory Players, 1940. Following the war has written many plays including The Lady's Not for Burning, Venus Observed, The Dark Is Light Enough; *also, translations from the French, such as* Ring around the Moon *(Jean Anouilh) and* Tiger at the Gates *(Jean Giraudoux).*

Bwlch, in South Wales, is difficult to reach without explicit directions and impossible to pronounce if you must ask any Welshman to guide you. When I finally arrived there, before a quaint old house, I was met by a very plain, friendly man with a puppy in his arms. ~ Trebinshwn House, as Christopher Fry calls his Welsh retreat, is devoid of electricity because the owner does not want it. I could make no interior photographs but took a few shots in the garden, mostly for the purpose of exploring my subject. Fry was not easy to explore. To any serious question he usually answers: 'Well, I'll have to think about it.' But he is not without humour, as you may know from his plays. When I asked him, for example, why plays customarily contained three acts he shot back, 'Because people like two intermissions.' Then, seriously, he added: 'Three acts—the first sets the problem, the second develops it, the third solves it.' ~ Having in mind the images of his own style of writing, I asked him whether Shakespeare could sell his plays to modern theatre managers. 'I think,' said Fry, 'he'd be asked to re-write them.' ~ As it was impossible to make a portrait at Trebinshwn House, we agreed to meet at Mr. Fry's house in London and meanwhile I went to see his play *The Dark Is Light Enough* which greatly delighted me. This second meeting in 1954 presented a new problem, not technical, but human, intensely and disturbingly human. ~ Halfway through our session the telephone rang. Mr. Fry answered it and spoke softly for a few seconds. He then announced that Marlene Dietrich had called to say that, as she had not previously met him, she was coming over immediately to remedy that situation. I went on with my work until the actress swept in and, ignoring everyone else, sat down at Fry's feet. 'You must not think you are my only love,' she began in her famous throaty voice, 'I have one other, Sir Alexander Fleming.' She went on talking to Fry in a low voice, quite oblivious of me and my assistants. The embarrassed playwright and the adoring beauty made an amusing tableau, but I fought off the temptation to record it on film. ~ At that moment Mr. Fry's mother, a lady of eighty-two years, was helped down the stairs by a secretary. She was determined to see Miss Dietrich. After giving the actress a smiling 'How do you do?' she climbed the stairs and I heard her say in a clearly audible voice: 'I didn't know that Christopher had risen so high in the world!'

MARTHA GRAHAM

American dancer and choreographer. Born in Pittsburgh, 1902; studied at Denishaw School of Dancing, Los Angeles, where she was later a student-teacher. Made first independent appearance in a dance recital, 1926; founded Dance Repertory Theatre in New York, 1930, and subsequently established Martha Graham School of Contemporary Dance in New York. Among her works: Primitive Mysteries, El Penitente, Errand into the Maze, Letter to the World, *and* Appalachian Spring. *Also, together with Agnes de Mille, has provided dances for* Oklahoma *and* Carousel; One Touch of Venus *and* Finian's Rainbow *included examples of Miss Graham's work.*

As everybody knows, Martha Graham has originated, out of the dance, a new art form. Naturally, I wished to photograph her in the posture and mood of the dance. But this seemed impossible under the circumstances. Upon arriving at Miss Graham's New York apartment in 1948 I was quite taken aback, though impressed, by the stark simplicity with which she had chosen to surround herself. On a modernistic table stood a grotesque piece of petrified wood, vaguely suggesting the attitude of a modern dancer. A rubber plant in one corner, a few pieces of very modern furniture, no pictures, no radio, no decorations of any sort—this, then, was to be the setting of a dancer's portrait. Then I looked up to the ceiling and it seemed only a few inches above my head. No one, not even Martha Graham, could dance in such a place. ∼ Compromise sometimes must be the stuff of which pictures are made. So, rather hopelessly, I sat Miss Graham on a low stool and asked her to assume various attitudes as if she had the space of a great stage around her. Amazingly enough, this restricted posture presented no problem, such perfect control had she over her body. She was sitting on a stool, in a low room, but she seemed to be dancing. In fact, she was dancing, and thus I recorded her. ∼ She talked to me about the dance but clearly with a single-minded devotion to her own type of art. Though it has won wide acceptance, she thought it 'went over' with younger people better than with older audiences. 'The young,' she said, 'have an appetite for experiment and experience, which is all that is really necessary. They have the habit of looking inside because of their concentration and study of psychology in schools today.' ∼ Martha Graham's new trend in dancing may be labelled impressionistic or given some other name, but it is certainly based on sound choreography. Yet where older dance forms often seem stilted, her dance is fluid and, therefore, it seems to me, more representative of this fluid and changing age. ∼ She submerges herself in her work utterly—even under a low ceiling and on a stool—so that she seems mentally and physically apart. Yet her art is never isolated from her audience. Like any art, it is lonely in creation but instantly communicates with all who watch it, as I, in an unlikely setting, watched it.

DAG HAMMARSKJÖLD

Secretary-General of the United Nations since 1953. Born 1905; educated at the Universities of Uppsala and Stockholm. Secretary of the Bank of Sweden, 1935; Under-Secretary for Finance, 1936-45; Chairman of the Bank of Sweden, 1941-8; Financial Adviser to the Ministry of Foreign Affairs, 1946-9, Under-Secretary, 1949-51, Minister, 1951-3; during this time was Swedish delegate at various economic conferences and negotiations with Great Britain, the United States, etc. Swedish delegate to the General Assembly of the United Nations, 1949 and 1951-3, before being elected Secretary-General.

As Secretary-General of the United Nations Dag Hammarskjöld holds the highest civil service post in the world, but he is also, in himself, a powerful political force. On his own initiative he is authorized to bring to the attention of the Security Council 'any matter which in his opinion may threaten the maintenance of international peace and security.' It is obvious that only a most unusual man could properly be entrusted with such enormous responsibilities. That Dag Hammarskjöld has met and even enhanced the prestige of his office is now universally agreed. ∼ As I entered the great glass rectangle on New York's East River in 1958 and went skyrocketting up the 'high rise' lift to the 38th floor I wondered just what kind of adventure was before me. What would be the man behind the official? ∼ In the large conference room that opens off the Secretary-General's office I was invited to make whatever arrangements I wanted. The room itself is simple, done in subdued browns and greys, with four or five modern paintings—two Picassos, a Léger, a Braque—the only decoration. The real drama of the room is centred on its western wall: a solid bank of windows with a breathtaking view of the spires and trenches of Manhattan. ∼ I was still busy with my preparations when a quiet voice asked me if I had everything I needed; Dag Hammarskjöld, unattended, had come into the room. Perhaps 'self-containment' is the term that best expresses the initial impression one receives of him—he is like an athlete who even in the stress of competition is in complete command of his faculties and holds added power still in reserve. An associate who knows him well told me that in the six years since Mr. Hammarskjöld was appointed he has known him to express anger only once, and even then, under great provocation, it was anger under control. ∼ The quality of self-containment has its physical expression as well. The S.G. walks with the grace and precision of a man whose muscles are as well controlled as his words. It is not surprising to recall that his chief outdoor activity was mountaineering. On the mantel of the drawing room in his New York apartment is an ice-pick—the pick that Tenzing held in his hand as he and Hillary placed the blue flag of the United Nations on the peak of Everest. ∼ I knew that before he came to the United Nations in 1953 Mr. Hammarskjöld in addition to being a distinguished economist and diplomat had been known as a patron of the arts and literature. I asked him if it was true that among English papers he always read the *New Statesman* but that he had said that he always 'started at the back' (the literary pages). He laughed and admitted that there might be some truth in this tale. He still reads contemporary verse; authors, artists, playwrights and actors—T. S. Eliot and Michael Redgrave for example—are among his chosen friends.

JULIE HARRIS

*American actress. Born in 1925 in Michigan; married Jay I.
Julien, 1946, and Manning Gurien, 1954. Studied at the Perry
Mansfield Theatre Work Shop, 1941-3, and the Yale Drama
School, 1945. Plays in which she has acted are* The Young
and Fair *(1948-9),* Magnolia Alley *(1949),* The
Member of the Wedding *(1950-1), and* I Am a
Camera *(1951-2); the last two were made into films and
she also appeared in the film* East of Eden.

Preparing myself, in 1956, to photograph Julie Harris, I watched her portray
Joan of Arc. Jean Anouilh's play *The Lark* had been in progress barely five
minutes before I forgot my camera, the theatre, and the actress. ~ Though
the stage is one of my loves and I have seen a great many plays, I do not
recall anything so moving as Miss Harris enacting the tragedy and the
triumph of the Maid. It would be a dull man who did not share her joy,
her anguish, her ultimate disillusionment with humanity. When she was
burned at the stake the watcher almost burned with her and felt her
conviction that the next world would surely be better than this one. ~ I
came out of the theatre exalted and limp. Next morning I awaited the
subject of my portrait, wondering whether she would bring with her some
of the evening's magic or whether, off-stage, Miss Harris would turn out
to be an ordinary woman who possessed only some remarkable histrionic
tricks. ~ The magic came with her. Though she seemed fragile, modest,
even girlish and shy, she turned my New York studio into a cathedral as
she recited some lines from *The Lark*. At once the spirit of Joan took possession of her and the mysterious power of her imagery possessed me also.
I hope that the camera conveys something of that moment and of this
woman's total immersion in the spirit of another, long dead. ~ It is often
difficult for a photographer to induce a mood of communication in his
subject and to catch it before it fades. Not so with Miss Harris. This supreme
actress could assume, or rather create, sustain, and truly feel any part,
tragic or gay. I marvelled at such talent in one so young and comparatively
inexperienced. A gift of this kind must come from the gods. ~ Everyone
feels her strange aura which is already becoming a legend of the stage. For
example, so the story goes, the immortal Sarah Bernhardt presented one
of her handkerchiefs to Helen Hayes and that great lady of the American
stage, though by no means old, passed the relic on to Miss Harris as the
actress who most deserved it. In her turn, Miss Harris unselfishly bestowed
the handkerchief on Susan Strasberg.

JASCHA HEIFETZ

Violinist. Born at Vilna, Russia, 1901, he began studying the violin at the age of three. Entered the Royal School of Music, Vilna, at five and graduated at nine. From there he was taken to St. Petersburg for further tuition. In 1917 he first played in New York. Heifetz is one of the world's best known and most highly respected virtuosi and has made some of the most successful recordings of works for violin; has appeared in many leading cities of the world.

The talent that has made Jascha Heifetz a great musician has not made him temperamental. I found him, at our first meeting in New York in 1945, quiet, cheerful, and hard-working. As he was writing music that day, he preferred to be photographed at his piano, on which he reverently laid his priceless violin. While I arranged my camera he talked with obvious knowledge about photography in which, I perceived, he is something of an expert. Nor is he one-sided in his own art. All types of music appeal to him and he once wrote swing, anonymously. During the last war, he recalled, he had played serious music for the troops but, as he put it with a chuckle, had 'rewarded' their attention by interpolating jazz into his programme. ~ I photographed Mr. Heifetz again in 1950 at his Beverly Hills home, and this time he was more willing to be portrayed with his violin, as a performer. How, I asked, would he define perfection in art? 'There is no such thing as perfection,' he replied, 'you attain a certain standard and then find out it is not good enough. If I play well, I always hope that next time I'll play better.' We fell to discussing appreciation of music among children and he offered a remarkably practical plan. 'Take a child's hands,' he suggested, 'guide them over the piano keys to pick out a well-known tune, and from that moment he will have a heightened interest in music.' Every child, he felt, should receive some musical education for his own enjoyment and satisfaction. With very rare exceptions, he added, children have a natural instinct for music which should be assisted gently but firmly. ~ What, I inquired, were the essential attributes of a great musician? 'Vitality, concentration, tact and stamina. One needs all these for the strenuous life of a concert artist.' A musician, I ventured to suggest, must be both 'delicate and sensitive,' but he dismissed these adjectives as quite inadequate to define a successful artist, who must have a strength of character to fulfil his talent. ~ This is no theory in Heifetz' case. He works with prodigious energy and under almost any conditions. A recording technician, after a lengthy session with Heifetz, observed in amazement: 'I don't know how he did it, but he was playing better after ten hours of recording than at the beginning.' ~ This story did not surprise me after I had seen the violinist at work and his calm search for perfection. If Heifetz, in his own mind, has not quite achieved perfection, the margin of failure was too fine for my ears.

ERNEST HEMINGWAY

American novelist and war correspondent. Born 1898; educated in elementary schools and abroad. Has used much of his personal experience in his novels and stories (of World War I in Italy as ambulance driver and soldier; the expatriate society of Paris in the twenties, when he met and was influenced by Ezra Pound and Gertrude Stein; the Spanish civil war, which he covered as newspaper correspondent). War correspondent in China, 1941, and on Western Front. His works include: The Sun Also Rises, A Farewell to Arms, For Whom the Bell Tolls, *and* The Old Man and the Sea *(Pulitzer Prize, 1953); all of these have been made into films. Awarded Nobel Prize for Literature in 1954.*

In his books and stories Ernest Hemingway has brought to life a swarming company of characters but has jealously concealed himself. After reading those tales of ferocity, violence, and physical suffering, I expected to meet in the author a composite image of his creations. Instead, in 1957 at his home near Havana, I found a man of peculiar gentleness, the shyest man I ever photographed. Therein, I imagine, lies the secret of his work. He has felt in his soul, with lonely anguish, the tragedy of our species, has expressed it in his writing, but, for self-protection, has built around himself a wall of silence and myth. ∼ Nevertheless, I wanted him to talk, to focus his mind, and hence his face, on some subject which would arouse both; so I asked him bluntly what he thought about that large tribe of writers who try to imitate his style. Forgetting his diffidence, he gave me a ready answer. The trouble with the imitators, he said, was that they were able only to pick out the obvious faults in his work; they invariably missed his real purpose and his real method—just as many readers remembered him chiefly for his defects. There was no bitterness in this remark, only a rather sad amusement. ∼ As he thought about my question I discovered that he had a wonderful smile—alive, kindly, and full of understanding. But on developing my negatives I liked best the portrait printed here. It is, I think, a true portrait, the face of a giant cruelly battered by life, but invincible. ∼ And what an astounding life this man has survived, quite apart from his work! He talked quietly about his airplane accidents. He was still suffering from injuries that would have killed most men. The worst of it was the doctor's strict diet. Perhaps he would soon be allowed more than a few glasses of wine every day. 'I don't drink while I write,' he added. 'You can't write serious stuff and drink.' I suggested that he must be quite unlike Churchill in that respect and he retorted: 'Churchill is a writer of rhetoric and to write rhetoric you must drink. But that's not my trade.' ∼ I tried to start him talking of his writing but was not successful. Once he had written a book, he said, it went out of his mind completely and no longer interested him. There must never be any residue from one book carried into another. Every book was a new challenge, I gathered, an experiment and an adventure. 'I must forget what I have written in the past,' he explained, 'before I can project myself into a new work.' ∼ As we were leaving, my wife noted some flowers growing between the stone steps of the garden. A gardener herself, she approved of flowers grown in this manner, though they disturbed the stones. 'Yes,' said Hemingway, 'but we can always replace the stones.' Between the rough boulders of this man's prose, I thought, the flowers of compassion will always grow, whether the public notices them or not.

AUDREY HEPBURN

British actress; born in Brussels in 1929. Member of the corps de ballet in Sauce Tartare *and* Sauce Piquante *in London's West End. Leading parts in American films* Roman Holiday *(1953),* Sabrina Fair *(1954),* War and Peace *(1956); has appeared in New York in the plays* Gigi, *1951, and* Ondine, *1954. Married Mel Ferrer, American actor, director, and producer, in 1954.*

I photographed Audrey Hepburn in 1956 in the Paramount Studios, Hollywood, where she was creating her starring role in *Funny Face*. I had seen her in various movies, and she did not surprise me in this meeting. I had expected to find her rather brittle, extremely sensitive, and always emotionally charged. So she is. Intensity, I suppose, is her particular quality and her particular success. Beauty is combined with an insatiable appetite for life, and for work too. ∼ Miss Hepburn was surprised and thrilled, as if I had offered her some extraordinary gift, when I said I would let her see my pictures before they were published—an unusual procedure in America. Accordingly, a few days later, I took the colour and the black-and-white pictures to her dressing room while she was having her hair shampooed. She greeted them with that explosive enthusiasm which the public has seen so often on the screen. 'What a relief,' she cried, 'to see pictures taken without foundation make-up!' I noticed then that, unlike most movie stars I had portrayed on my trip to Hollywood, Miss Hepburn was comfortable with only a line of eyebrow pencil and some lipstick. Her natural beauty requires little assistance from the art of make-up.

MAURICE HERZOG

French mountaineer; leader of party to make first ascent of Annapurna (26,493 ft.) in the Himalayas in 1950. Born in 1919 in Lyons; an officer in the Chasseurs Alpins, saw active service 1939-42, 1944-5. Started climbing at the age of sixteen when he spent holidays at Chamonix; made some notable ascents in the French Alps. Lost all his toes and several fingers through frost-bite in conquest of Annapurna; had to undergo nearly three years of treatment and rehabilitation. The book entitled Annapurna, which he subsequently wrote by dictation, proved a best seller. Determined to return to mountaineering, in 1952 he reached the summit of the Matterhorn.

It is hard to say exactly what sort of man I expected to find in Maurice Herzog, but I did imagine that he would be big, burly, and tough, for he had climbed Annapurna. ∼ My conception of mountain climbers, as I saw at once, was far off the mark. The man who greeted me in his Paris apartment in 1954 was extremely handsome—the type of a diplomat. He did not look rugged, but rather delicate, with the poised strength of coiled steel, and he had the eyes of a mystic, a visionary. I seemed to detect in him a secret flame, the fierce energy of a dream which drove him on adventures incommunicable to others. ∼ He was friendly, however, and quite unpretentious. If I thought it necessary for the portrait, he said, I could photograph his hands, badly frozen in the Himalayas. This I thought unnecessary, but I liked him for his candour and simplicity. ∼ Of course my first question to Mr. Herzog, the obvious layman's question, was whether he believed in the Abominable Snowman? 'Well,' he said, 'the thing that caught the fancy of the world was the use of the word "man." I don't believe in the existence of such a "man" but some kind of very large bear living in the high altitudes is a possibility. A bear, not a monkey. The animal would need very thick fur. Anyway, expeditions are searching for the Abominable Snowman, so called, and it will be very interesting to hear their findings.' ∼ At this point I noticed, in a place of honour, a tea urn draped with a white muslin veil. Yes, said Mr. Herzog, there was story here. The veil had been given to him by the sherpa who accompanied him on the Annapurna climb. It was a good luck charm and he must never part with it since the talisman was powerful only when in his possession. I could see that he valued it highly, not for its magic but for its memories. ∼ I ventured to suggest that his experiences on Annapurna had been of great value to the Everest expedition. He agreed, but quickly added, 'Of course mountain climbers always pass along every bit of information and give one another all the help they can.' ∼ Though I knew the question to be futile, I could not refrain from asking him if he could put into words his feelings as he conquered his mountain. 'Oh yes,' he said, 'that experience was real enough, shaking, in fact, but it is impossible to describe it in words. At such a time there must be a great depth of feeling you know, for after all, it is a grave moment in a man's life.'

HIS HOLINESS POPE JOHN XXIII

262nd Supreme Pontiff of the Roman Catholic Church, elected to the Papacy November 1958, on the death of Pope Pius XII. Angelo Guiseppe Roncalli was born in 1881, son of a peasant farmer in Lombardy, North Italy. Studied at seminary in Bergamo; later won scholarship to the Pontifical Seminary, Rome. Ordained, 1904; returned to Lombardy as secretary to Bishop of Bergamo and as a teacher at the seminary. Served as Chaplain in Italian army during World War I. Made an Archbishop, 1925, and given first diplomatic assignment—Apostolic Delegate in Bulgaria; promoted to Nuncio, 1930; sent to Turkey and Greece as Apostolic Delegate, 1934; appointed Nuncio to France, 1944; permanent observer of the Holy See to UNESCO, 1952; returned to Italy on being made a Cardinal in 1953 as Patriarch of Venice.

Having photographed Pope Pius XII and happily produced his favourite portrait, since distributed in millions of copies throughout the world, I was naturally eager to put on film the rugged, manly features of his successor, Pope John XXIII. ~ Once again, however, my task was made more difficult by the fact that His Holiness could spare only a little time from his many duties. Arriving in Rome on December 27, 1958, I was unable to photograph His Holiness until January 2. Meanwhile, however, I was invited to attend a Baciamano (literally, hand-kissing), a ceremony which included only twenty-four persons, in the Hall of Tapestries. We all kissed the Holy Father's ring and he, in turn, had appropriate words for each of us. Then he blessed us from the centre of the room saying 'Let me offer you a collective benediction that you may take it with you and share it with all those you meet in any part of the world.' Afterwards I attended a General Audience in the Clementine Hall where the Pope addressed a large gathering from his throne, with the aid of a microphone, in Italian. I asked one of the nuns what he had talked about and she replied with a smile, 'About his youth.' That same afternoon I found myself in the Hall of Benedictions listening with fascination to Handel's *Messiah* presented by the Opera House of Venice, the city of which Pope John was Archbishop and Patriarch before his election. He was carried to the concert on his sedia and I noted that he had a special word of acknowledgment for his bearers. ~ By this time I had formed a clear and, I think, accurate impression of His Holiness as a compelling personality, a simple, forthright human being, a theologian of genius no doubt, but a man among men and already, I should suppose, a major figure in the long history of his Church, to which he has brought, even at his advanced age, an extraordinary power of leadership, and also of imagination. ~ That impression was confirmed when, after several nights of worry, I arrived at last in his presence and went to work. Speaking in French, I recalled a newspaper headline, 'Le Pape est en prison' (The Pope is in prison). That report, referring to his recent visit to convicts, seemed to amuse him. Then, as the time was ticking away very slowly from the Vatican's point of view, and very swiftly from mine, His Holiness asked me whether I was not tired. 'No, Your Holiness,' I said, 'but very anxious.' So I was, until the portrait was finally printed at my studio in Ottawa. As I left him, he imparted his blessings with a spontaneous, fatherly smile, adding 'Bene, bene, bene.' Placing his hands on my shoulders he said, 'I wish you to enter into your diary that you have had the longest visit with Pope John to date.'

AUGUSTUS JOHN, O.M.

The English portrait painter Augustus John may seem somewhat melancholy, grim, and alarming in my portrait. That quality of brooding remoteness is one side of him and no doubt lies close to his genius. But our meeting in 1954 was warm and gay. One of those afternoon teas was served that are the glory of old England, and at it Mr. John's charming wife presided in their Hampshire home. ~ What, I ventured to ask, did he think of portraiture by film as compared to canvas and brush? 'Well, of course,' he said, 'they are quite different media. You can't fairly compare them. Yet both in their own ways are capable of great things. But then, you know that already. You have proved it with your camera.' ~ He made it clear that he had little use for most contemporary painters. The old masters are his idols. Michelangelo, Raphael, Rubens, Rembrandt—he spoke of them with candid idolatry. 'These great men,' he added, 'liked best to portray the common man.' So does John, as his portraits show. When I compared his simple yet powerful drawings to those of the immortals, he stood up suddenly in the middle of our sitting, bowed deeply and, with a comic flourish, announced: 'No greater honour can be paid to any artist.' ~ Luckily I seemed to have said just the right thing to produce the mood of relaxation and rather wistful contemplation that I wanted to record—the look of the man who sees his own private visions of beauty behind the faces of his subjects. At any rate, he was an ideal subject and our time together passed far too quickly. ~ It was getting late and I had to take my leave. At the door Mr. John put his arm around my shoulders and said a little plaintively, 'I wish I could offer you some further hospitality.' Already he had offered me much. But the thing I would remember was the simple integrity of the artist, his devotion to his own ideals of art, a master's loyalty to the artists of the past. He has followed his own path and, I think, he has followed it alone, quite undisturbed by modern fashion and inwardly happy with his quest.

CARL GUSTAV JUNG

Swiss psychologist; born 1875. Docent, Zürich University, 1905-13; practised as psychologist-physician; studied particularly the new system of psychological testing known as the 'association method'; a founder of International Psychoanalytical Society, 1911; resigned 1913 at time of break with Freud. Professor of Psychology at the Federal Polytechnical University, Zürich, 1933-41, and at the University of Basle; resigned in 1945 to concentrate on research and writing. Has written extensively on psychology; latterly has had a particular interest in the implications of psychology and its relationship with religion. His works include: Two Essays on Analytical Psychology, Psychology and Religion, The Integration of Personality, Psychologie und Alchemie, Mysterium Coniunctionis.

A photographer must be an amateur psychologist of sorts but in the presence of Dr. Carl Jung, at his home in Zürich in 1958, I felt somewhat at a disadvantage. However, the 'poet of the mind,' as Jung has been called, turned out to be very human, and his conversation (which I noted down) provocative. I began by asking him if we were over-emphasizing psychology in modern society. 'Oh no,' he said with a rather impish little smile, 'quite to the contrary.' Was it true, as some people had said, that modern man had become psychologically diseased? 'Modern man,' he replied, 'is as rational and as crazy as he ever was. But we're rattled these days. Things are going too fast and too far. Science is only man's honest attempt at understanding. There's no end to the various aspects of psychology. Only their totality makes possible an approximate cognition. But no cognition has ever increased the sum total of well-being, because every Good is paid for too heavily.' ∼ How, I asked, did a psychiatrist cope with his own psychological problems? 'Yes, how indeed?' said Jung. 'He copes, like everybody else, as well as he can, that's all. And it's usually deplorably enough.' ∼ Why were there so few renowned women psychiatrists? 'Intellect,' he said, with another smile, 'isn't their long suit as a rule you know. And true love, their long suit, is invisible.' ∼ When I told him that America was obsessed with psychiatry and yet often unstable, almost at times hysterical, Jung retorted: 'America obviously needs a lot of psychiatry. Therefore everybody talks about it, and makes it cheap, common, vulgar. No wonder it doesn't work there.' No, he did not intend to visit America. It had too many people. He preferred to think in the quiet of Switzerland where, he said, his neighbours respected his privacy. ∼ Yes, he agreed with the title of James Thurber's book *Leave Your Mind Alone,* but unfortunately, he remarked, 'the mind is not discreet enough to leave you alone . . . that's the trouble.' ∼ I said I would make an unsatisfactory patient for the psychiatrist because I gained my happiness through my work. 'Ah,' he answered, 'the secret of happiness is unhappiness because man has fear, sadness and shadow over his life. Those who seek happiness can never find it. It's extinguished when you seek it. You should wait till it comes, like the arrival of a guest late in the evening.' The present age, he went on, was full of unhappiness. 'The structure of the world has never before been so split. The pressures of our time have forced us to create a private Iron Curtain of our own. Alas, the United States and Russia are unfortunate lovers.' ∼ Many great men of science, I ventured to say to yet another of my subjects, do not believe in God. 'True,' said Jung, 'but that doesn't injure God.'

HELEN KELLER

Born in 1880 at Tuscambia, Alabama, she has as a result of illness been completely blind and deaf since the age of nineteen months. On behalf of the blind has lectured extensively all over the world and holds many awards for her work in relief of the handicapped. Her books include Helen Keller's Journal *(1938) and* Let Us Have Faith *(1941).*

On first looking into the blind but seeing eyes of perhaps the greatest woman in our world, I said to myself: 'The light comes from within.' And what a light of courage shines through the face from the dauntless soul of Helen Keller! ~ Katharine Cornell, her devoted friend, had taken me to Miss Keller's apartment in New York, in 1948, and explained the ritual of our meeting. The woman who has no sight or hearing shook my hand and then placed her marvellously sensitive fingers on my face. In her mind's eye, I knew, she already had me completely photographed. We were *en rapport* and I could make my portrait. Although I could speak to Miss Keller only through Miss Polly Thomson, her faithful companion, who dials braille into Miss Keller's palm, we soon developed a code of our own. At the slightest pressure of my fingers on her hand, she knew at once exactly which way I wished her to turn and at what angle I wanted her head. Her extreme sensitivity, her alert mind, her kindness and understanding, but most of all her gaiety, kept me amazed throughout the whole sitting. ~ Sight and hearing had passed into her hands. Therefore a portrait of the hands was as important as a portrait of her face—hands that create light out of darkness, sound out of perpetual silence, and alone bring this woman into communion with nature and her own kind. So I photographed those hands and as I looked at the result I repeated my first observation of Miss Keller: the light did indeed come from within. ~ Our sitting finished, I said to her, 'You wouldn't know, but this is not the first time I have met you. One of my earliest attempts to read English, years ago, was an article in the *Reader's Digest* called 'How to Appreciate the Beauties of Sunset.' You wrote it. Now, having met you in person I shall no longer think of you in terms of sunset but of sunrise!' 'How I wish,' she quickly replied, 'that all men would take sunrise for their slogan and leave the shadows of sunset behind them.' That chance remark, it seemed to me, told the story of Helen Keller better than a library of books. By her incredible victory over the flesh she had left the shadows behind her. Blind, she had seen the sunrise; deaf, she had heard the music of the spheres. I left her with a new sense of our human possibilities.

WANDA LANDOWSKA

Harpsichordist; 'responsible for renaissance of the harpsichord and true interpretation of 17th and 18th Century Music.' Born in Warsaw, 1879; studied the piano from the age of four. A graduate of the Warsaw Conservatory of Music. She has resided in the United States since 1941 but is a French citizen. Founded School of Ancient Music at St. Leu la Forêt, France, 1927. She has also made concert tours in Europe, Africa, Asia, and the Americas.

When possible, I like to discreetly observe my subjects and study them from a distance, in their own surroundings, before I photograph them at close range. Thus, to form an impression of Wanda Landowska, I went to Town Hall, New York, in 1945, and listened to one of her concerts. She played, of course, divinely. I was eager to put this remarkable artist on film and I felt sure that my task would be easy. After my long experience, I should have known better. ∼ Madame Landowska's living room, where the portrait was to be made, filled me with foreboding from the start—a beautiful apartment to be sure, a fit setting for an artist, but a grand piano and two harpsichords left me no room to manœuvre in, hardly enough space for my camera and lights. That was not the worst of it. Madame Landowska is an imperious person, used to her own way. So, no doubt, am I. At that moment she was surrounded by a host of little protégés who ran about rather like scared rabbits at the lady's bidding. How could I hope to make a portrait, or anything more than a hasty snap-shot, in such surroundings? ∼ However he may fare at other times, a photographer must be the mental master of the situation when he is at work, even if his subject is the illustrious Madame Landowska. But I almost despaired of mastering her, the crowded apartment, and the restless children. Then it occurred to me that anyone who could play Bach as she played it must be more than a technical virtuoso. She must be a great woman and therefore a woman of understanding. When I intimated my difficulties and the necessities of my craft, she understood at once. After that we both forgot the cluttered room and the somewhat fractious atmosphere.

LE CORBUSIER

Le Corbusier is a pseudonym for Charles-Edouard Jeanneret, French architect; born in 1887. Constructed his first building at the age of seventeen. One of pioneers of modern architecture and town planning, he planned large sections of cities of Buenos Aires, Stockholm, Antwerp, Algiers, Nemours (Africa), and Bogotá, also the entire new city of Chandigarh (capital of the Punjab). Has been town and country planning consultant to numerous governments in Europe, Asia, Africa, and America, and has published a number of works on urbanism. Commdr. de la Légion d'Honneur.

When I arrived at his home in Paris in 1954 to photograph him, Le Corbusier, one of Europe's greatest architects, who had recently built a large new town for the Government of India, at a cost of millions, was leaning against a spiral staircase which, he said, had cost him only two hundred dollars. Le Corbusier was very proud of that staircase and its small cost. All his works, large or small, were evidently precious to him—so precious, indeed, that he seemed to regard them almost as personal secrets. ~ He received me graciously and co-operated fully in the making of his portrait, but in conversation he proved depressingly reticent. The reticence was deliberate and, I concluded, habitual. This man had been so much abused and so often misrepresented in the press and the public mind that he did not intend to discuss his controversial views on architecture lest he be further misquoted and misunderstood. I did learn, however, that Le Corbusier is devoting a good deal of time to painting and is not averse to discussing a side of his work which, I take it, is not controversial. He was especially proud that one of his paintings had recently been purchased by the National Gallery in London. ~ The sitting went well enough, photographically, but gave me little knowledge of the architect's mind. So I did my best and left him with his staircase and I know not what plans for loftier works of shattering originality, certain, I imagine, to make him always a controversial figure—if a silent one.

DAVID LOW

British caricaturist. Born in New Zealand, 1891; educated in Christchurch, New Zealand. Has been political cartoonist for the Christchurch Spectator *(1902); the Sydney (Australia)* Bulletin *(1911); the London* Star *(1919),* Evening Standard *(1927-50) and* Daily Herald *(1950). Joined the* Manchester Guardian *in 1953. Works include:* Cartoon History of Our Time, Europe since Versailles, Low's Autobiography.

Not only as a peerless craftsman but as a shrewd judge of mankind, David Low had long fascinated me. What, I wondered as I prepared to meet him in 1943, lay behind the cartoonist's changing moods of iconoclasm and warm compassion? As I had suspected from his visible work, Low, who seems to despair and rejoice by turns as he surveys the human scene, turned out to be a philosopher disguised as a newspaper artist. ∼ In his bantering whimsical style—the Low conversation and written word bearing the same gay signature as the famous cartoons—he gave me his considered definition of human greatness. Though a little sceptical of public reputations, which he has often punctured wholesale, Low said he had found plenty of greatness in our age, but it was seldom of the highest sort. 'I see lots of the smaller greatness lying about, I mean the people who are very good at the exercise of their talents, but I find very few who have even a touch of the greater greatness—the understanding of life and their fellows. My own direct experience narrows me down to only a handful: Gandhi, Franklin Roosevelt, Churchill at times, Shaw and Wells.' His analysis of these men, too long to be reported fully here, was at once kindly but surgical. Each had his failings. Yet in all of them failure and mistake were swallowed up in victory. ∼ Where, I asked Mr. Low, did he find his never failing source of ideas, the impish magic of his cartoons? 'I can't really answer that,' he said. 'Even habit has something to do with it . . . a mysterious process. I used to walk across Hampstead Heath every morning and by the time I reached a certain bush I usually had an idea. Another stimulant is the sound of running water in my bath tub. In the old days the top of an open bus seemed to provide a queer inspiration. Relaxation? I relax by driving a car and in the cinema where once a day, between half past six and eight o'clock, I just sit and enjoy someone else's work.' Evidently Low had made a deep study of the cartoon as an art form and an instrument of politics. The earliest known cartoon, he told me, was scrawled on the pavements of Rome to ridicule the early Christians. In ancient Egypt, he said, the artists were under the direction of Toth, the God of Expression, and their political notions, if they had any, were curbed by the priests. The Greeks mainly acted satire instead of drawing it. ∼ I asked Mr. Low how much understanding he assumed in his readers. 'A reasonably intelligent interest in the matters of life and death around us,' he replied. 'Naturally, I key my assumptions somewhat higher among readers of thoughtful newspapers than among those of the popular amusement-*cum*-sport papers.' ∼ How effectively did cartoons mould public opinion? 'That depends,' he said, 'on the cartoons. But potentially a cartoon can be as influential as a poem, a speech, a text, a piece of music, or an essay. Who can measure such an influence?' ∼ As you see, when I photographed Low in 1943, he was enjoying some experience of his own, chuckling over his private version of Lenin and the Russian Revolution.

NORMAN McLAREN

Canadian film-maker. Began making films at art school in Scotland with second-hand film and borrowed camera. Worked for John Grierson's G.P.O. Film Unit in London directing 'live' films and making animation shorts. Came to New York, 1940. Joined Canadian National Film Board; trained and set up animation department; has travelled to China and India to teach techniques of animation and sound. His films include: a series based on Canadian folk songs and Begone Dull Care, Blinkity Blank, Neighbours, A Chairy Tale, Le Merle. Has won numerous awards for his work.

The young man in this portrait of 1957 is looking through a strip of film on which he has painted what I take to be a dancing hen. In fact, Norman McLaren, the artistic prodigy of the Canadian National Film Board, is looking, through his own private prism, with his own peculiar angle of refraction, at the gorgeous, humorous, and tragic spectacle of life. The results of his observations are known the world over. By painting on film and scratching his strange music directly on the sound track he has produced a unique art form. ~ After I had photographed him at the National Film Board's Montreal headquarters, I wrote Mr. McLaren to ask various questions about his work. The reply, in his handwriting, would make a family heirloom. All the capital letters are alphabetically legible, more or less, but each is conceived in a weird drawing of birds and beasts unknown on land or sea. He can't help it; he thinks in pictures. ~ But, like most artists of the highest talent, Norman McLaren is unable to explain his work. 'It's true,' he wrote (in a jungle of winged creatures), 'that I do sometimes make use of the very things that people try to avoid most. In film making, for instance, scratches and dust are two things that must be avoided at all cost on the photographic negative. But I have often been entranced by the intermittent flickering, fluttering, sputtering, and joggling of the scratches during the projection of an old, beat-up film. Sometimes, if the film was poor, it was definitely more entertaining to watch the scratches than to watch the film. So I decided to make a whole film with nothing but scratches.' (Those scratches, as he calls them, became the classic *Blinkity Blank*.) ~ McLaren depends mainly on his subconscious, seldom knowing when he starts how a film will end, but he is not above making use of mere accident. For instance, when he was painting the film of *Begone Dull Care*, one of the strips fell to the floor while wet and, as he thought, was spoiled. On projecting it, however, he found that the wet dye had receded in a small circle from each dust speck, making a pleasant, over-all pattern. 'From that moment,' he said, 'we became experts in dust, eagerly collecting it in small packets from all kinds of surfaces, and classifying it by the kinds of effects it would produce when sprinkled carefully on wet, dyed film.' ~ I asked him if his methods could be applied to long, feature pictures. He thought they could be, but his own interest lay in the short, the medium which has made the Canadian documentary film esteemed everywhere.

ANNA MAGNANI

Italian film actress. Born 1908; separated from her parents at an early age, she was brought up by grandparents in a poor district of Rome; at 17 she went to the Academy of Dramatic Art and then into many touring companies, supplementing the meagre income from these engagements by night club appearances where she specialized in Roman street songs. Began film career in 1934 with The Blind Woman of Sorrento; *at the end of the war Rossellini saw her acting in revues for soldiers and in 1946 gave her the leading role in* Open City. *First came to United States for première of* Bellissima, 1953. *Other films have included* Before Him All Rome Trembled, The Rose Tattoo (*for which she won an award from the Academy of Motion Picture Arts and Sciences in 1955*), *and Renoir's* The Gold Coach.

The greatest actress in Italy, perhaps the greatest in the current world, has a reputation for artistic temperament and human fury. Yet her reply to my cable from Ottawa, before I left for Europe in 1958, came the same day. Yes, Miss Magnani would gladly give me the time I needed at her Rome apartment. ∼ At our photographic session I endeavoured to explore behind the famous features and the brooding, almost overwhelming air of tragedy. In conversation I found that, as on the stage or on film, she is always Magnani. And that, I suppose, is the secret of her art. ∼ I began by asking her if it were good for an actress to work in Hollywood. 'It's good,' she said, 'to work anywhere, provided you have a good script and a good director. But above all it's essential to work where people understand and appreciate you.' ∼ She preferred, she said, to act in her own language, Italian, but English was good, too. 'The first time I played in English a miracle happened . . . everything went well.' Everything always went well with her, I suggested, but she said it was never that easy. 'I have always played parts that are very demanding and almost border on madness.' ∼ She was rather sad, however, about the Italian movies. 'We had a kind of realism, in such movies as *Open City* and *The Bicycle Thief*, which no one could imitate. It was new and original. Then the Italian cinema started to imitate the Americans, to rely for its success on sexy girls, Cinemascope and so on. It lost most of its distinctive qualities and became something hybrid, anonymous.' ∼ 'Why did I go on the stage? Because of unhappiness, perhaps. I wanted to do so many things. I didn't know I had talent, only that I exploded with ideas . . . like firecrackers. I was never sure which way they would go.' She protested, however, that she was never difficult with her directors. 'With a good director,' she said, 'one never fights. . . . The best directors today are Kazan, David Lean, and Fellini. But no matter who the director may be, the first time I play a scene is always the best. I can never equal it again.' ∼ 'Oh yes, the improvements in movie techniques can be useful, especially the big screen. Think how wonderful the scene of my death in *Open City* would have been with Cinerama! I dying in the middle of the street and all the people around me.' ∼ 'My greatest role,' she told me, 'was in *The Human Voice* . . . I'll never be able to do it again. You will see why when we screen it for you tomorrow.' ∼ I did see what Miss Magnani meant. In this unique work by Cocteau she plays entirely alone, the whole action concentrated in a telephone call. No other living actress, I dare say, could so concentrate the gamut of human emotions, but Magnani could do this and doubtless still greater things. Many more firecrackers, we may hope, have yet to be exploded.

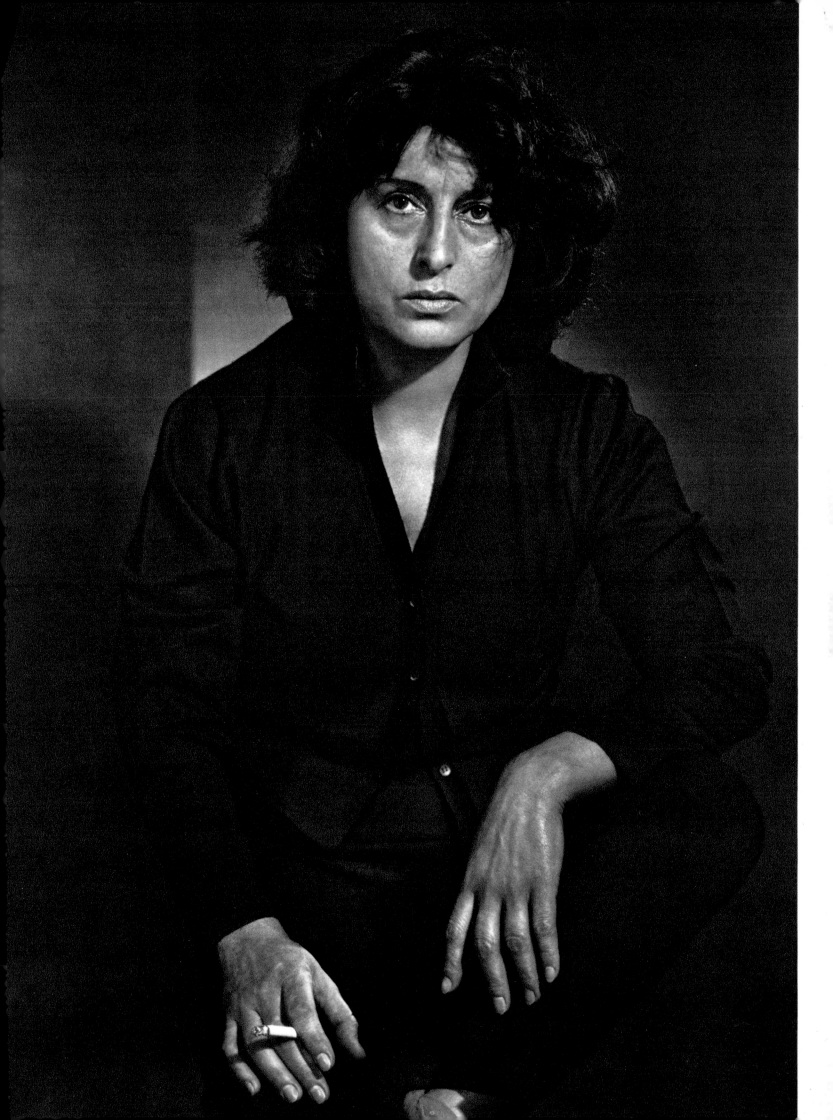

ANDRÉ MALRAUX

French author. Born 1901; studied archaeology and orientalism; served with Republicans in Spanish Civil War; served in World War II, when he was wounded and taken prisoner; he escaped in 1940. Minister of Information 1945-6. In 1958 he again became Minister of Information in the De Gaulle government. He later relinquished this post to become Minister of State, dealing with matters of general public interest. Publications include: La Condition humaine *(for which he was awarded the Prix Goncourt, 1933),* L'Espoir *(film),* Goya: Œuvres complètes, *and* Les Voix du silence.

After reading of his incredible adventures, physical and spiritual, as soldier, revolutionary, communist, anti-communist, writer, and philosopher, I expected to find in André Malraux a remarkable person. When I met him in Paris, in 1954, we talked about archaeology, one of the many subjects in which he is a master. Our conversation ranged far that day while we sipped a glass of champagne and reflected on the past. ∼ In his drawing room I observed an arresting Graeco-Buddhist statue of a bodhisattva and I decided to photograph him with this relic. Closer inspection revealed a curious resemblance between the owner's profile and that of the statue. When I remarked on this fact, M. Malraux retorted, with an impish delight, 'Archaeologists devoted to their subject always end up by looking like the works of art they have discovered. In Egypt, one looks like the ancient Egyptians, in central Asia like the Graeco-Buddhist, in Mesopotamia like the Sumerians.' Then he added with a smile: 'That's true, except in the case of the man who discovered the "Winged Victory of Samothrace"!' ∼ He was particularly interested in recent discoveries revealing a new language and a whole civilization in Persia. That prompted me to ask him whether the peoples of Asia might eventually take over the leadership of the world, say after the year 2000. He replied that Russia would never become the world's leader, but he was not willing to say the same about China. It had made tremendous strides in a very short time and was still moving rapidly. ∼ What about Germany? 'There's no need to fear Germany as a world conqueror,' said the man who had fought so gallantly in the French Resistance. 'The Germans have tried at various periods of history, but they have never succeeded in world conquest. Charlemagne was certainly no fool, neither was Bismarck, but neither they nor the Kaiser, nor Hitler, ever succeeded. There's a trait in the German people, though they are a great people, that precludes the possibility of their ever becoming world conquerors.' ∼ He did not attempt to forecast the future of the United States. He observed, however, that it was the first world leader which had never sought power but had had greatness thrust upon it. ∼ Who, I asked, was the most important figure of our century? M. Malraux believed that, without question, Lenin had changed the world more than any contemporary. But despite Lenin's materialistic dialectics, he thought that the world might witness, before long, a religious revival. 'Not necessarily of Christianity,' he added, 'but of perhaps a completely new religion. Then it may be that the man of the whole century could turn out to be Gandhi, and India would again enjoy a period of great illumination, radiating over the whole world.'

THOMAS MANN

German novelist and essayist (1875–1955). At the age of twenty-five he wrote Die Buddenbrooks, a novel portraying the decay of a family over several generations. It made him world famous and is now considered a classic. It was followed by Der Tod in Venedig, Der Zauberberg, Joseph und seine Brüder (a tetralogy), and many masterly short stories. Awarded the Nobel Prize for Literature, 1929. Escaped with his family from Germany, 1933; deprived of German citizenship, 1936; in 1938 began a long residence in the United States; went to Switzerland, 1953; died in Zürich, 1955. His last published book was Bekenntnisse des Hochstaplers Felix Krull. Most of his works have been translated into English.

Many critics would say, and doubtless with good reason, that the late Thomas Mann was the greatest literary figure of his time. I confess, however, that when I encountered him in an orange grove near Los Angeles in 1946 I knew nothing directly of his work. I had come ill prepared to photograph him; had, in fact, read none of his books. Nevertheless I was soon aware, at first hand, of the quiet, massive, and purely Germanic power of the man. ~ He received me in his garden, under that blazing California sun which he had found so pleasant as an exile from Hitler's Germany and his boyhood home on the Baltic. It was a great joy, he remarked almost naïvely, to be able to pick one's own oranges just outside the door. Then, with old-fashioned and rather formal courtesy, he ushered me into his well-stocked library, his wife in close attendance. They had known each other since school days, he told me, and I found the attachment between these two elderly people very moving. ~ Before we began work Mann offered me coffee and cognac, served with the formality which, I supposed, was customary in that old European home from which the Nazis had driven him. He began to speak, with a quiet flattery, of my work. Especially he had noted my portrait of Artur Rubinstein to whom he referred as 'that civilized man.' The adjective was interesting. I think it describes Mann himself exactly. ~ As we got to work on his portrait he appeared thoughtful, said very little, but when he did speak it was in a voice peculiarly gentle and kindly. He seemed to have an especially soft place in his heart for the United States, where he had been so warmly welcomed in his exile, and obviously relished the climate, the scenery, and the spacious freedom of California. ~ I received a strong impression of Mann's sincerity and deadly earnestness. Here, I thought, was typical cold German efficiency and concentration illuminated, as in Goethe, his idol, by a sudden warmth and flash of sunlight. ~ I had been intrigued throughout the sitting by the writer's hands. They seemed to reveal both his strength and his delicacy. I therefore made some studies of the hands alone and eventually, when I submitted my pictures for Mann's inspection, he sent me back a letter which is one of my most prized possessions. 'The study of the hands,' he wrote, 'is a highly remarkable piece of work and reminds me of a drawing by Albrecht Dürer.' Mann, I think, would have made an excellent subject for Dürer, who admired men of power.

MARCEL MARCEAU

French mime. Born in Strasbourg, 1923; studied at the Ecole des Beaux-Arts in Paris and was a pupil of the famous actor and teacher Charles Dullin; soon after he created his own company, the Compagnie de Mime Marcel Marceau. Appeared at Paris theatres where his success led him to undertake a tour overseas; has now been seen on several tours in the United States and Canada.

From the start everything went badly in my attempt to photograph Marcel Marceau, the great French mime. I had arranged a sitting in Montreal, in 1956, where I would stop on my way to the United States, but at the appointed hour I found that all my equipment had been shipped, by mistake, straight through to New York. However, some weeks later, M. Marceau arrived in New York for further stage appearances and a new appointment was set in my studio-apartment. I felt, after the Montreal fiasco, that I owed my subject unusual politeness but, in my efforts to please him, let the situation get entirely out of hand. ∼ The actor had his own preconceived ideas about the portrait he wanted. In fact, as I was about to conclude the sitting I suddenly realized that I had been recording all those familiar poses, attitudes, and expressions that I had seen on the stage. To avoid doing this I had already asked him not to use his white-face make-up, so that I could see the abounding mobility of his own face. Thus, in the concluding moments, I was compelled to be quite firm with him. Though he may have doubted their wisdom, he took my suggestions well. ∼ M. Marceau has very definite theories of art and some particular preferences. He is particularly enamoured of his portrayal of 'Death' in his famous sketch, 'Youth, Maturity, Old Age, and Death,' and feels that at the end of this sequence he really dies and leaves this world! I think he almost believes it as a fact. ∼ In the course of a long, random conversation, he told me an amusing story about his son Michel, then seven years old. He had become his father's most ardent admirer and at the conclusion of every performance led the applause with shouts of 'Bravo, Papa, bravo!' M. Marceau warned the boy repeatedly that this sort of thing was not done, yet invariably, as the curtain descended, the father heard the son's small familiar voice. He told me that it was highly embarrassing, but I could see that he loved it. ∼ The actor may fancy his role as 'Death,' but my favourite in his diverse repertoire is 'The Butterfly.' In it he seems 90 per cent butterfly, 10 per cent human being (or is it *vice versa*?) and I always think of him thus, flitting through life with a butterfly's delight plainly visible on that ever changing sensitive face.

THE RT. HON. VINCENT MASSEY, P.C., C.H.

Governor-General of Canada since 1952. Born 1887; educated at the University of Toronto and Balliol College, Oxford. Lecturer in Modern History, University of Toronto, 1913-15. President, Massey-Harris Co., 1921-5. Minister without Portfolio, 1925; attended the Imperial Conference, London, 1926, with Canadian delegation; (first) Minister Plenipotentiary for Canada in the United States, 1926-30. President, National Liberal Federation, 1932-5. High Commissioner for Canada in the United Kingdom, 1935-46; a Trustee of the National Gallery, London (1941-6; Chairman, 1943-6), and the Tate Gallery (1942-6); Chancellor, University of Toronto, 1947-53; Chairman, Canadian Royal Commission on National Development in the Arts, Letters and Sciences, 1944-51; Chairman, the Massey Foundation.

As Governor-General of Canada (the first Canadian to hold that post) Mr. Massey is set apart from the struggles of politics that rage outside the walls of his residence in Ottawa. But there is far more to this man than the ceremonial personage who represents the Queen of Canada, the bonds of the Commonwealth, and the long history of the Canadian people on both sides of the Atlantic. Mr. Massey is also, of course, a great man and a profound thinker in his own right. He would have achieved distinction in any career that he might have followed and was, indeed, an eminent public servant long before he became head of the state. ∽ This photograph was taken in 1952. My first meeting with him took place many years previously and sticks in my mind, being marked by a notable phrase. I had gone to Government House, in 1933, when Lord Bessborough was Governor-General. As I arrived (a young and very frightened photographer in his first professional year) I saw two gentlemen walking arm in arm down a long corridor. They were talking with animation and one of them said, 'We are the victims of our own intelligence.' That, it seemed to me, described quite adequately the dilemma of our time. The two gentlemen turned out to be Mr. Massey and his friend, the late Colonel Henry Osborne, but I did not venture to ask which of them had coined the phrase. Recently, as a guest at one of His Excellency's dinners, I recalled the earlier incident. 'That's a good phrase,' said my host, with a twinkle, but he did not enlighten me further. I think, however, that it was Mr. Massey who had remarked on the dangerous intelligence of the human race, for intelligence, in all its aspects, has been the great concern of his life. ∽ The Governor-General's intellectual eminence, his high taste in literature and all the arts, his completely civilized air, are a formidable thing at first sight but I know no kinder or more sensitive man. He is equally at home among the great in a drawing room or the lumberjacks in a northern camp or the Eskimo of the Arctic, and he has made it his business (often at serious hardship and sometimes real danger) to see every aspect of his sprawling, diverse nation. I doubt that any Canadian knows the nation better in a physical sense and few have understood its many-sided mind so well. ∽ Only the other day His Excellency said that, to his great regret, there seemed to be fewer and fewer eccentric people, heretics, and non-conformists in the world; it was the unusual individual, he added, that made the world go round. He is certainly among that shrinking company.

WILLIAM SOMERSET MAUGHAM, C.H.

*British novelist and dramatist. Born 1874; educated King's
School, Canterbury; Heidelberg University; and St. Thomas's
Hospital, where he studied medicine. His novels include:*
Liza of Lambeth, Of Human Bondage, The Moon
and Sixpence, The Painted Veil, Cakes and Ale,
The Razor's Edge. *He has written also many plays, some
of which have become classics of the modern theatre:* The
Circle, The Letter, The Constant Wife. *His brilliant
short stories are very popular today and have been the basis of
several films. He now divides his time between his villa in the
south of France, a house in South Carolina, and a suite at the
Dorchester Hotel in London.*

The face of Somerset Maugham—a deeply lined, wise, and almost ageless face—is as familiar to the world as are the writer's teeming works. Yet the man I discovered in the grand suite of a New York hotel in 1950 entirely surprised me. He was quite unlike the man I had expected from reading his stories and many articles about him. ~ Apparently he had kept his appointment with me by interrupting his customary afternoon nap. The black eye-shield he wears at such times still dangled from his hand. Though he obviously would have preferred to rest (for he is now an 'old party' as he is always telling reporters), he gave me his whole attention and almost charmed me away from the business of the sitting. ~ To begin with, his face is arresting—not handsome, of course, in any conventional sense but impressive, rather like the carved, wooden image of some tribal god in the South Seas where he has roamed so often. The eyes are penetrating, almost hypnotic and intensely alive. That well-known expression of starkness (often taken for cynicism) breaks frequently into the most engaging smile. To my surprise Maugham, the realist, the hard-boiled sceptic, possessed an irresistible warmth. This made the work of the camera easy but did not help my other purpose. I wanted to ask him a thousand questions about his methods, his life, and his views, but after half an hour I realized that I, not he, was being interviewed. Out of long habit, I suppose, he automatically begins to draw a stranger out. His curiosity about human nature is insatiable in his old age. He finds in everybody, even the chance passer-by, the possibility of some quirk or anecdote that has in it the making of a tale after passing through the alchemy of his imagination. I had the sudden vivid feeling that he viewed the human comedy with the objectivity of my camera. ~ At any rate, Mr. Maugham talked little and I am afraid that I talked much, simply because I could not resist a man who appeared to have no interest in the world just then but me. Doubtless that is his custom with everyone who crosses his path and the result is known to just about everyone who reads his stories. ~ Mr. Maugham was not in a talking mood that day, but I have heard that in this respect his mood can change. A close friend of his remarked to me, later on, that Maugham 'when he gets going is an extraordinarily interesting talker and talks as well as he writes. Yes, and he reads his stories aloud as well as any actor could.' ~ I remember Somerset Maugham, then, rather as a polished, elegant, and sympathetic listener, with an immense cunning in penetrating another man's innermost thoughts.

FRANÇOIS MAURIAC

French poet, playwright, and novelist. Born 1885; brought up in strict Roman Catholic orthodoxy by his widowed mother, educated at Bordeaux University and the Ecole des Chartes in Paris. His first literary success was Le Baiser au lépreux, *published in 1922. Other works include* Génitrix, Le Nœud de vipères, Asmodée *(a play), and* Le Sagouin. *During World War II he worked for the French Resistance and wrote a 'Cahier noir' for the clandestinely published* Editions de minuit. *After the war he contributed to* Figaro, Figaro littéraire *and* La Table ronde. *Won the Grand Prix of the Académie Française, 1926, and the Nobel Prize for Literature, 1952.*

It is quite absurd—I speak with strong conviction and somewhat bitter experience—to say that the French are a decadent race. How can they be when so many of them climb six flights of stairs several times a day? Indeed, most of the great Frenchmen whom I have photographed choose to live on the sixth floor, or higher, without an elevator—François Mauriac, the eminent and devout Catholic writer, for example. Such stamina and asceticism would be unthinkable in the vigorous New World. ~ Since M. Mauriac could not be asked to come down from his Olympian heights, I and my assistant were compelled to ascend, with all our heavy photographic equipment, in several breath-taking climbs. And then, after all the wires had been connected, there was no electricity! So we waited hopefully, on that day in 1949, for the Paris power to be turned on again. ~ Since he lives by choice under such difficult conditions, I was not entirely surprised to find M. Mauriac sunk in profound pessimism. Apparently he saw nothing to encourage him in the state of the world and was entirely convinced that civilization must ultimately face a third, devastating war. He spoke in a strange, muffled voice, which he explained as the result of an operation. ~ While we waited for electricity, he talked freely on many subjects of a philosophical sort. I deliberately needled him a bit on his familiar journalistic feud with Sartre and the existentialists, then the prevailing fad in France. M. Mauriac was most definitely anti-Sartre, whom he considered an apostle of negation, a very bad and dangerous state of mind to be nourished among the French people. Evidently M. Mauriac had done his best to discourage this movement and, with an air of triumph, he showed me a newspaper article in which, it appeared, he had entirely vanquished Sartre. ~ We had been talking for a long time but still there was no electricity and I was on the point of despair. Yet after climbing those endless stairs with all my photographic paraphernalia I did not intend to leave empty-handed and undergo the same ordeal a second time. ~ On the off chance of success, I placed my subject before an open French door and against the greyest of Parisian skies. My assistant removed a sheet from the bed and held it up as a reflector. The resulting profile portrait, I feel, conveys François Mauriac's Gallic charm and perhaps something of his dark despondency about human affairs.

GIAN CARLO MENOTTI

Italian composer. Born in Italy, 1911; came to United States, 1928; educated at Curtis Institute of Music, Philadelphia. Member of the teaching staff of Curtis since 1941. Won Guggenheim Award, 1946 and 1947, and Pulitzer Prize, 1950 and 1955. Compositions include the operas Amelia Goes to the Ball, The Telephone, Amahl and the Night Visitors, The Old Maid and the Thief, The Medium *(also filmed),* The Consul, The Saint of Bleecker Street, Maria Golovin, *and a ballet,* Sebastian. *Has written all his own libretti, and the libretto for Samuel Barber's opera* Vanessa.

In an age of specialization, it is a pleasure to come upon a person who has explored all aspects of the field to which his special talent contributes. Such a person is Gian Carlo Menotti. A man of music and of letters, he has also been producer and director of his own works, and in Paris on one occasion even hung the American-made stage-sets which had proved too much for the stage-hands. ～ I photographed Mr. Menotti in 1956 at his home in Mount Kisco, New York. Here with the poet Robert Horan and the composer Samuel Barber he shares a house, three grand pianos, and several paintings by Braque, Modigliani, Picasso, and Berman. That the arrangement has been a happy and fruitful one was recently shown by Menotti's writing of the libretto for Barber's opera *Vanessa*. ～ Quiet and courteous, Mr. Menotti has nevertheless passionately adopted the defence of contemporary American composers. Accusing the Metropolitan Opera of being 'not an audience, but a habit,' a 'museum,' he has affirmed that the general public has better taste than it knows and that it wants to hear new works—and he has a telling argument in the success of his own operas. ～ Though he cheerfully admits that at seventeen he was a 'spoiled brat,' made lazy by too much adulation in the salons of Rome, the experience of gaining his later education in the United States, where he was both ignorant of the language and unknown, has transformed him into a modest, hard-working, constantly developing individual. A few years ago, at Town Hall, he gave us some insight into this new attitude in the following words: 'Hell begins on the day when God grants us a clear vision of all that we might have achieved, of all the gifts which we have wasted, of all that we might have done which we did not do. The poet shall forever scream the poems which he never wrote; the painter will be forever obsessed by visions of the pictures which he did not paint; the musician will strive in vain to remember the sounds which he failed to set down on paper. There are few artists whom I can imagine resting in heavenly peace: Leonardo, Michelangelo, Goethe, and a few minor artists who have merited that peace. But, for the weak, the lazy, the damned—their torture shall be the more horrible in proportion to the greatness of the genius they have wasted. For me the conception of hell lies in two words: TOO LATE.' Mr. Menotti, I am sure, will never deserve such condemnation.

HENRY MOORE, C.H.

On a bitterly cold and rainy English morning in 1949 I found myself in Henry Moore's studio. The temperature seemed low both physically and spiritually. Those huge sculptured figures in plaster expressed, for me anyway, a certain cold objectivity in the man who had made them. Clearly, Moore knew exactly where he was going, what he intended to do, and would not be distracted by any criticism. Of course, he has been frequently criticized for his stark and simple masterpieces, but no sculptor of our time has been so widely imitated. ∼ As I looked at the carvings and plaster casts in that freezing studio, I was baffled. An unschooled eye such as mine could not detect, in many of the works, what the sculptor meant. Yet I soon found that this ultra-modern and heretical artist had a deep reverence for the sculptors of the past on whose work, I suppose, he has built his own. When I asked him who was the greatest sculptor of all time he replied without hesitation: 'Michelangelo!' I asked what reception Michelangelo would receive if he were alive today. Mr. Moore gave me a thin smile. 'Michelangelo,' he said, 'would find much more competition.' ∼ I ventured to suggest that conservative views seemed to control most of the exhibitions of sculpture today. 'Oh yes,' he said, 'conservatives will always resent anything new . . . until it is generally accepted. Then they accept it too.' ∼ He told me that his major works, especially the very large ones, were always carved in the open. Only under the sun and sky did he feel the close affinity of sculpture to nature. He liked best to see his work displayed in the open, as part of a landscape. 'I'd rather have a piece of my sculpture put in a landscape, almost any landscape,' he said, 'than in the most beautiful of buildings.' ∼ A layman is more likely to remember Moore's creations mainly for the gaping holes drilled through many of them. I mustered enough courage to ask him about these arresting apertures. 'The first hole made through a piece of stone,' he said, 'is a revelation. A hole can have as much shape and meaning as a solid mass.' ∼ I glanced up at the family group, here pictured, and began to understand a little better what he meant. ∼ By this time I was chilled to the marrow and gladly accepted the sculptor's invitation to his home where a blazing fire and a hot cup of tea made me feel less like a figure in stone myself. We were surrounded here by many small bronze sculptures and I found these welcome and ready companions.

GILBERT MURRAY, O.M.

British classical scholar and philosopher; born in 1866 in Sydney, Australia; died in 1957. He came to England at the age of eleven. Educated at Merchant Taylor's School and St. John's College, Oxford. When only twenty-three was appointed Professor of Greek at Glasgow University which post he held for ten years; Regius Professor of Greek at Oxford University 1908-36. His career has been devoted to the translation of Greek drama into English and the fostering of its return to the English stage, to works on Greek literature, and to leadership in the movement for international union. Chairman, League of Nations Union, 1923-38, and afterwards Co-President.

A bright English morning in 1955 found me on the road to Oxford, but I went with a feeling of private trepidation. How did one approach a man said to be perhaps the most scholarly of our age? ~ I found him in the perfect scholar's setting. His beautiful library was flooded with golden sunlight and, of course, with the aura of Oxford's past. The man himself was also warm and sunny, but he spoke little. As in all great men of my acquaintance, simplicity seemed to be his dominant quality. I noted a typewriter of antique design in a corner where, no doubt, his works of scholarship were produced. And on the floor beneath his table there was a crude electrical heater against the winter chill of England. Though not an Englishman by birth (he was born in Australia), he had taken to the ways of England and was almost as much a fixture in Oxford as its buildings. ~ At that moment he was busy with a speech to be delivered at the celebration of his ninetieth birthday. I could see that it was no time for prolonged conversation and, besides, I was not equipped to meet him on his own ground of learning in a sanctuary where learning has flourished for so long. I asked him but one question: What was the secret of his longevity? The aged man gave me a brisk, businesslike reply: 'Keep mentally occupied and, I would like to think, an inner serenity.' This man's mind had been fully occupied for nearly a century, he was still busy, and in a chaotic age he was utterly serene. I left him with a new serenity of my own.

EDWARD R. MURROW

American television and radio broadcaster. Born Greensboro, N.C.; educated at Washington State College. President of the National Student Federation, 1929-32; Assistant Director of the Institute of International Education, in charge of foreign offices, 1935-5; with Columbia Broadcasting System since 1935, as Director of Talks and Education (1935-7), European Director (1937-46), war correspondent (1939-45), Vice-President and Director of Public Affairs (1945-7); now Director, reporter, news analyst, and conductor of television programmes (Person to Person, See It Now). Has lectured in United States and abroad on international relations.

Not many men of our time are as familiar to the public of North America as Edward R. Murrow. We have all seen him, heard him, and made up our minds about him. Yet the man who sat before my camera was not, it seemed to me, the well-known figure of the television screen. To begin with, Murrow looks rather frail on television, invariably harassed and wrinkled with thought; his tall, athletic figure is usually lost, in his public appearances, because he slouches deeply in his chair, and his eyes are puckered not by anxiety or by stage fright, but by the glaring studio lights. In life he is over six feet tall, an outdoor man who was brought up in the West Coast woods and hates big cities. ~ Edward Murrow is an exceedingly modest man and his idiom in private conversation is relaxed and easy. Still, there is an earnestness about him. He feels his responsibility as one of the leading reporters of human events in our time. That sense of integrity explains, among his other adventures, the celebrated encounter with the late Senator McCarthy. Murrow's respect for the truth was outraged and he let himself go. ~ On the lighter side, one of the most amusing pieces of Churchilliana was recounted to me by Murrow during our meeting. Apparently once he invited the then British Prime Minister to make a gramophone record for commercial sale and Mr. Churchill remarked, 'Murrow, I would be distressed if you were to take a financial risk.' Then he quickly added: 'Murrow, I neglected to say that I would be equally distressed if you were to profit considerably without my participation.' Murrow has a keen memory for such anecdotes, and a sharp eye for great men's weakness and strength. At the close of the sitting he repeated for me his expression of one contribution of Churchill to the war effort. 'Churchill was the man who marshalled the English language and sent it into battle when we had little else.' ~ Some time after I photographed him in 1956, I corresponded with Murrow about his philosophy of reporting. In reply he said that he believed 'that radio and television have an obligation to expose the listener and the viewer to the realities of the world in which he lives, and if those realities are harsh or unpleasant, that is not the fault of the medium. It should be the effort of television to hold a mirror behind the nation and, indeed, the world, and to expand the horizon and pique the curiosity of the viewer.' At the same time we should remember that 'there is no such thing as a truly objective reporter. We are all prisoners of our own reading, travel, experiences and acquaintances. No man can eliminate his prejudices but he may recognize them and attempt to discount them when writing or talking.'

JAWAHARLAL NEHRU

Prime Minister and Minister for External Affairs, Republic of India, since its inception in August 1947. Born 1889; educated at Harrow and Trinity College, Cambridge. Barrister-at-Law, Inner Temple, 1912; joined Gandhi's non-violent non-cooperation movement in 1920; from then on actively associated with all movements aiming at Indian independence; imprisoned eight times for political activities. Succeeded his father as President of the Indian National Congress in 1929; President also 1936, 1937, 1946, 1951-4. Vice-President, Interim Government, 1946.

Seven years elapsed between my first portrait of Jawaharlal Nehru, in 1949, and the second, in 1956. In that period, despite the cares of office and the Indian statesman's extraordinary schedule of daily work, he had changed little. The slight figure remained athletic, the delicate, ascetic features alert with sensitivity and yet with an iron determination. Few men among the great of this age have impressed me so much as this interpreter of the Western and Asiatic worlds. ~ If Mr. Nehru is philosopher, statesman, and practical politician by turns, and no doubt a giant in history, his mood is often playful. He knows how to relax. If he did not, he would have collapsed long ago from his customary time-table of eighteen hours' work a day. Before he starts the day's business, he told me, he invariably performs the traditional exercises of yoga. ~ At our second meeting he greeted me, in Government House, Ottawa, with mischievous severity. 'Mr. Karsh,' he said, 'you have not kept your promise to visit India. I am disappointed in you.' 'Mr. Prime Minister,' I replied, 'as soon as I can afford the luxury of putting aside six months of my time, I shall avail myself of the opportunity to see your colourful land. It does not take long to know the leaders; it takes much longer to know the common man.' 'You are right,' he replied, 'with all my experience I cannot claim to know India myself.' ~ As we prepared to make the portrait, Mr. Nehru chatted freely about many things and we immediately found a subject of common interest. Like me, he is fascinated by photography. Before the responsibilities of government interfered with his hobby he constantly carried a Leica hung around his neck and, on a recent visit to Bali, had found in the folk dancers there a delightful subject for his camera. Everyone in Bali, he told me, was an exponent of the dance. ~ When I recalled his ready answers at a recent gruelling press interview in Washington, he remarked, 'All political questions are the same. They don't require any clairvoyance.' Then he answered my question about the possible settlement of the Kashmir problem. 'I am an advocate of peace,' he said, 'and by the method of peace this and all other problems must be solved.' As to the deep schism between the United States and Russia, he remarked that 'in this world it's impossible and unnecessary to have a meeting of minds, to the extent of 100 per cent, in order to get along, as we must.'

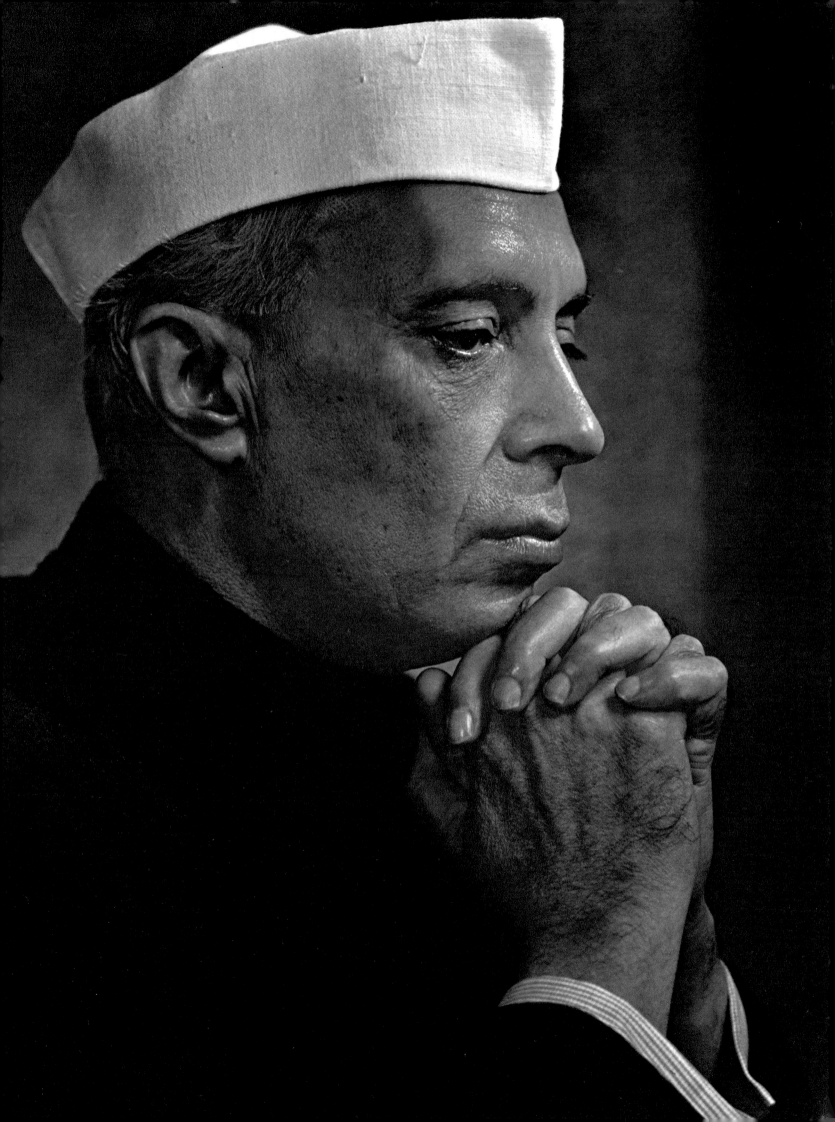

GEORGIA O'KEEFFE

American artist. Born 1887 in Sun Prairie, Wisconsin. Studied at Art Institute of Chicago (1904-5), Art Students' League, New York (1907-8), University of Virginia (1912), and Columbia University (1914-16). Commercial artist, 1909; supervisor of art for the public schools of Amarillo, Texas, 1912-14; instructor in art, University of Virginia, summers, 1913-16; head of art department, West Texas State Normal College, Canyon, Texas, 1916-18. Has confined activities to painting since 1918. Became one of a group (including Marin and Dove) sponsored by the photographer Alfred Stieglitz, whom she married in 1924. Paintings first exhibited by him at 291 Fifth Avenue, and later at the Intimate Gallery and An American Place. After her husband's death in 1946 she spent 3 years cataloguing his collection and distributing it to major centres in the United States. Since 1949 has lived in New Mexico. Best known as a highly original and daring flower painter, she is represented in the Tate Gallery, London, the Metropolitan Museum of Art, New York, and the museums of Brooklyn, Cleveland, Detroit, Springfield, Mass., and Washington, D.C.

'At last, a woman on paper.' These were the words uttered by Alfred Stieglitz when he first saw the drawings of the artist Georgia O'Keeffe, whom he was later to marry. When I came to Abiquiu, New Mexico, in 1956 to photograph this remarkable woman who has so enriched American art, I expected to find some of the poetic intensity of her paintings reflected in her personality. Intensity I found, but it was the austere intensity of dedication to her work which has led Miss O'Keeffe to cut out of her life anything that might interfere with her ability to express herself in paint. Her friend and fellow artist Anita Pollitzer has commented perceptively on Miss O'Keeffe: 'A solitary person, with terrific powers of concentration, she is so in love with the thing she does that she subordinates all else in order to win time and freedom to paint. . . . She has worked out a simple, well-considered pattern of life, so unvaried that the average person would refuse to live it, and she refuses to allow anything to pull her away from it. People figure very slightly in her world. . . . Her decisions as to her use of time are very definite. Last year [1949] she said to me: "I know I am un-reasonable about people but there are so many wonderful people whom I *can't take the time* to know." She says that even in her student days she saw that dancing at night meant daytime lost from painting—so she refused to dance although she loved it. She decides carefully on each point, what to have and what to give up. There is nothing weak about her willpower. I have never known her to have any regrets or envy.' ~ As though to concentrate her vision inwardly Miss O'Keeffe has banished colour from her surroundings. Her adobe home, with wide windows on every side overlooking the mountains, and almost completely empty of ornament, seemed stark to me, but when I asked Miss O'Keeffe why she chose to live in such a remote area she replied, 'What other place is there?' In the end I decided to photograph her as yet another friend had described her: 'Georgia, her pure profile against the dark wood of the paneling, calm, clear; her sleek black hair drawn swiftly back into a tight knot at the nape of her neck; the strong white hands, touching and lifting everything, even the boiled eggs, as if they were living things—sensitive, slow-moving hands, coming out of the black and white, always this black and white.'

SIR LAURENCE OLIVIER, KT.

British actor-manager. Born 1907. First appeared in Shakespearean play at Stratford-on-Avon in 1922; since 1929 has appeared in London, New York, Paris, and other cities in Shakespearean and other roles; co-director, Old Vic Theatre Company, 1944-5, toured with this Company in Australia and New Zealand, 1948. Actor-manager at St. James's Theatre, London, after 1950. Has played in many films, including Wuthering Heights, Rebecca, Pride and Prejudice; *produced, directed, and starred in film versions of* Henry V, Hamlet, *and* Richard III. *Married to British actress Vivien Leigh.*

When Sir Laurence Olivier greeted me at his London home in 1954, he appeared fatigued. Small wonder, since he had been directing and himself acting in his film production of *Richard III* all day long. Besides, he said, he had been wearing a false nose and various other uncomfortable disguises which converted a handsome contemporary Englishman into the hunchback villain of feudal times. ∼ Sir Laurence, and his *petite* wife, Vivien Leigh, made a charming couple and did not grudge me their time even though they were packing for their departure next day to California. ∼ Soon after the sitting began, their Siamese cat named Boy leapt upon Sir Laurence's head and completely obscured his face . . . obviously a privileged character of the household. I snapped a few candid pictures of this frivolity to remind me, later on, of a great actor mastered by a pet which alone could steal a scene from him. ∼ Presently, while I waited for the right moment for my portrait, Sir Laurence began to talk about the photography used in *Hamlet*. The magnificent depth of field in this film, the sense of grandeur, of distance and mystery were due, he said, to the use of a special lens and to highly imaginative lighting. (He did not mention, of course, the depth, grandeur, and mystery of his direction and acting.) A play like *Hamlet*, he added, was much better filmed in black and white than in colour, for colour would undermine the atmosphere of high tragedy. ∼ Several years later, I had an opportunity to meet Sir Laurence again, when he was performing in John Osborne's play *The Entertainer* on Broadway. I had wondered why so great an artist had agreed to act a rather sordid part, created by one of England's 'angry young men.' Sir Laurence saw the play in another light. He said he greatly admired Mr. Osborne's work; in fact, it had been written especially for him, at his own request. ∼ I asked him if he felt that the angry young men were significantly affecting the English drama. 'Undoubtedly,' he said. 'But the term "angry young men" is a feeble press epithet and a misnomer. Some of the critics are greatly distorting the fine work of these playwrights. I think they are definitely contributing something to the stage, in form, in content, and in action.' ∼ When I asked him what difference he found in British and American audiences he gave me a quick reply: 'I could think of much, much more pleasurable ways of finishing my career than by answering that one!' What, I said, did the movies offer to the serious artist? 'From experience among my friends I would say that financially it is fairly all right in both fields and the choice would be entirely one's own inclination. For myself I enjoy both the theatre and the film media equally but I should say as a general rule that the film is the director's medium and the theatre the actor's medium.'

ROBERT OPPENHEIMER

*American physicist. Born 1904; educated at Harvard,
Cambridge, and Göttingen. Professor of Physics, University
of California and California Institute of Technology, 1929-47;
Director, Los Alamos Laboratory, New Mexico, 1943-5;
Chairman, General Advisory Committee to the Atomic
Energy Commission, 1946-52; Director, Institute for Advanced
Study, Princeton, since 1947.*

Dr. Oppenheimer greeted me warmly, in 1956, at the Institute for Advanced Study, Princeton. He remembered that we had met briefly before and now he had left an important conference to keep our appointment. But I detected in this famous scientist a certain brittleness and I thought that the record of deep suffering was written plainly on his face. After his experiences, this was hardly surprising. ~ However, he proved most cooperative and, at my request, wrote down the names of six scientists whom he considered the world's most outstanding. Then, after he had finished, he smiled and added, 'If you asked me for a list tomorrow, most likely I'd give you a different one. Anyway, some of the greatest men of our calling have died recently.' He particularly regretted the untimely passing of Enrico Fermi. ~ But the atmosphere of that sitting was not all sombre. For I had noticed with fascination an oddly shaped pork-pie hat hanging on a peg, the last sort of hat you would expect to see on the head of a sober scientist. The story of that hat tells us something of the other Oppenheimer. He had been presented, he told me, with one of those huge ten-gallon cowboy hats from Texas and, thinking the brim far too wide, had cut it down with a pair of scissors. The result could hardly be called a sartorial triumph. I was happy to see, however, that this scientist, harassed by personal difficulties and by his knowledge of mankind's peril from the discoveries of science, could make a joke of his own. Indeed, I asked him to wear this whimsical headpiece. He did so with a laugh and I photographed him thus to record the thinker's lighter side. ~ But I was aware, of course, that the world of Oppenheimer, behind the genial smile and schoolboy joke, was something like a hundred light years away from my world, or that of any layman. One has only to read some of his simpler speeches and essays to see that this man is probing not only for a knowledge of scientific phenomena useful in our daily life but for ultimate truths explaining the mystery of all life. I could appreciate, however, his blunt dictum on the future of man's life if human intelligence did not catch up with the march of weapons. 'Far beyond disarmament,' he has said, 'one has to envisage a world of affirmative collaboration in the world's work between people irrespective of nationality . . . the world has to be an open world in which, practically speaking, secrets are illegal.' ~ To such a world Dr. Oppenheimer has made, not without great sacrifice, his own unique contribution.

146

YUKIO OZAKI

Japanese statesman (1858–1954). Educated at Keiō Gijuku School and Engineering College. Editor-in-chief of the newspaper Niigata Shimbun (1870) and later joined the Hōchi Shimbun; appointed counsellor of the Foreign Office (1897) and Minister of Education in the Ōkuma-Itagaki Cabinet (1898); later resigned; elected Mayor of Tokyo (1904); appointed Minister of Justice (1915). From the first general election (1890), was elected to the House of Representatives twenty-four consecutive times. Often referred to as the 'father of parliamentary politics' for his parliamentary career which lasted almost half a century.

By those who should know I had been told, and could well believe, that Yukio Ozaki was one of the most significant men in the modern life of Japan ... not only a great and courageous man in his own life, but a symbol of deep, agonizing changes in Japanese life. As a democrat, a pacifist, and an internationalist, he represented the earliest stirrings of democracy in his country and, though often jailed, sometimes exiled, and constantly threatened with assassination, he never wavered for a moment in his faith, or in his love for America which, as he said, stood for everything he had sought in his own country. ～ It was with a sense of reverence, therefore, that I approached the old man—he was in his nineties at the time, in 1950, and had just concluded a tour of the United States. The Dewitt Wallaces, of *Reader's Digest*, had asked me to photograph him and the sitting took place in New York in the Waldorf Towers. A wonderful gentleness and an almost saintly look brooded on Ozaki's face. But they were not easy to catch on film. ～ Evidently he heard my words with difficulty. His daughter acted as a competent interpreter and as she leaned towards his ear to transmit some amusing remark his countenance lighted up with an oddly childlike expression. It was then I made my picture. ～ Ozaki lived on to the age of ninety-five. I never saw him again, but whenever I am in Washington at blossom time, and look at the Japanese cherry trees there, I remember that he gave them, when he was Mayor of Tokyo, to the American people... a living memorial to his faith in human freedom.

MADAME RANJIT S. PANDIT

Vijaya Lakshmi Pandit, Asia's most experienced woman diplomat and the sister of India's Prime Minister Jawaharlal Nehru, is at present High Commissioner for India in the United Kingdom. Madame Pandit was born in 1900, and educated privately. She was married to Ranjit S. Pandit in 1921. For participation in Indian national movements she was imprisoned in 1932, 1940, and 1942-3. Minister of Local Self-Government and Public Health, 1937-9, 1946-7. India's Ambassador to Moscow, 1947-9; to Washington, 1949-51; and to the United Nations, 1951-4. From 1953 to 1954 she was President of the U.N. Assembly, the first and so far the only woman ever to have held this position of honour and influence.

About Indian women there is a beauty of a very special kind—calm, serene, untroubled by the stresses of a speed-mad Western world. That kind of beauty illuminates the face and, I think, the life of Madame Pandit. ~ She has achieved a career which must be unique among women. She has represented India, since its birth as an independent nation, in Moscow, in Washington, at the United Nations, and in London. ~ There must have been, I thought, some special influence in this woman's life, apart from the unfailing support of Mr. Nehru. I had guessed correctly. Over the luncheon table in Washington in 1949, Madame Pandit revealed the mystical touch and inspiration of Mahatma Gandhi. 'He taught me,' she said, 'that no one could ever harm or hurt me, except myself.' That simple lesson has been, I imagine, the foundation and touchstone of all her work. No one could harm or hurt her, except herself, and with that knowledge she has maintained, with courage and never with dismay, her long struggle against racial discrimination, her vision of the dignity of all men. ~ When the photographic session was over I thanked her for being so patient, gracious, and co-operative. She waved all that aside. 'It is my brother,' she said, 'I would like you to portray. And *he* does make an excellent subject.' So, soon afterwards, he did. But the fame of the brother could not overshadow in my memory the peculiar radiance of the sister.

LESTER B. PEARSON

Leader of the Liberal party in Canada since 1957. Born 1897; educated at the University of Toronto and St. John's College, Oxford. On teaching staff of the University of Toronto before joining Canadian Department of External Affairs in 1928; Ambassador to the United States, 1945; Secretary of State for External Affairs 1948-57; Canadian representative to UNRRA meetings, 1944-6; Senior Adviser, Canadian Delegation to San Francisco Conference, 1945, and Canadian representative at subsequent meetings of the U.N. General Assembly; Chairman, U.N. Political and Security Committee during Special Session of the General Assembly, 1947, and again at 4th Session, 1949; President, 7th Session of the General Assembly, 1952; Canadian representative signing North Atlantic Treaty, 1949; Chairman, North Atlantic Council, 1951-2; Chancellor, Victoria University in the University of Toronto, 1951–; Nobel Peace Prize, 1957.

Quite apart from his political career and even if he had never held elected office Mr. Pearson would qualify, I think, for any list of the world's leading thinkers. Moreover, the man whom all Canadians and most foreigners know as 'Mike,' is an artist in his way, an artist of humanity, whose canvas is our battered civilization, whose long-sought composition is peace. With his political activities, in a partisan sense, I am not here concerned. He has always fascinated me by his activities in other fields, especially the non-partisan conduct of foreign affairs . . . at long and at short range, as a public man, and as a fellow townsman of Ottawa. ∼ When I first met and photographed Mr. Pearson, in 1944, he was Canada's Minister to Washington. 'You make me,' he wrote, 'look almost like a statesman.' In fact, my various portraits make him look, I hope, only like the always boyish and sometimes tortured human being that he is. The second adjective may seem strange but I have watched his face, as photographer and friend, too long to miss the clouds that occasionally fleck the familiar sunshine. ∼ The award to Mr. Pearson of the Nobel Peace Prize in 1957 was a source of pride to all Canadians regardless of party. I was present in the House of Commons as he received the congratulations of his supporters and opponents alike. His appearance that day stuck in my memory and I resolved to capture it, in a permanent portrait. The likeness printed here, against the background of the Commons chamber, reproduces, I believe, his appearance on that memorable occasion . . . a blend of confidence and humility, the secret iron behind the outward geniality. ∼ Afterwards I submitted a series of questions to Mr. Pearson in the hope of probing, as it were, his philosophy of international life. I was particularly interested by his interpretation of Canada's position amid the constantly changing problems of the world. 'Canada can always take a disinterested stand, in the sense that she can do what is right irrespective of what anybody else does. This is easier for us because we have no national interests that are continually under examination or challenge at the United Nations. So we do not need to feel superior or smugly virtuous. We have also to remember that in cases of doubt as to what is right or wrong—and most international issues involve doubt in this sense—we have always to take into consideration the importance of co-operating with our friends. We should never break with them unless we are absolutely sure we are right. On the other hand if we follow the United Kingdom or the United States automatically, any influence we have with them or in the international community would soon disappear.'

WILDER PENFIELD, O.M., C.M.G.

*Canadian neurologist. Born Spokane, Washington, 1891;
educated at Princeton, Johns Hopkins, and Oxford Universities
(Rhodes Scholar, 1914). Has held posts at Columbia
University, Presbyterian Hospital, and New York
Neurological Institute, Vanderbilt Clinic. Professor of
Neurology and Neurosurgery, McGill University, Canada,
and Director of Montreal Neurological Institute, 1934-.*

A tragic coincidence explains this portrait of Dr. Penfield, the world-famous neurological surgeon of Montreal. ∼ I had already taken various portraits of him alone, but I wished to photograph him with his colleague Dr. William Cone and his assistants. They had planned a clinical meeting in the laboratory of the Neurological Institute one afternoon in 1952, and I grasped the chance to make a group portrait including two great humanitarians of our time. ∼ Everything seemed to be turning out well. My camera and lights were in place. The doctors and technicians had taken their seats. I was ready to begin when Dr. Penfield was called hurriedly out of the room. I waited impatiently for his return, but when he appeared some minutes later I realized at once that he had received bad news. His face indicated shock and grief. In a low voice he said 'John is dead.' Everyone in that room seemed to be stunned. John, I learned later, was their favourite orderly, a veteran of more than a quarter of a century in the Institute. While preparing to go home, and in the act of putting on his coat, he had collapsed and died before anyone could reach him, of a heart attack . . . an ailment which neither Dr. Penfield nor any of his colleagues had ever suspected. ∼ I had not foreseen, of course, a situation both tragic and dramatic which seemed at first to make photography impossible that day. Nevertheless, by unconscious reflex, I snapped the camera shutter. The resulting photograph shows Dr. Penfield at a revealing moment. To me it represents the great surgeon's love of humanity, his interest in humble folk, his deep devotion to his work of preserving human life. It shows also his sorrow, the sorrow perhaps of all doctors when they realize, as they must realize so often, that in the end their ancient adversary must always win. ∼ Earlier, when photographing him alone, I remarked that he did not look unlike a monk, a man living among and chastened by human suffering. And I ventured to ask him if doctors in general were pious people. He said somewhat wryly that piety was not their strongest point. That opinion, I think, is denied, so far as Dr. Penfield is concerned, by his look in a mood of intense sorrow and pity for humankind.

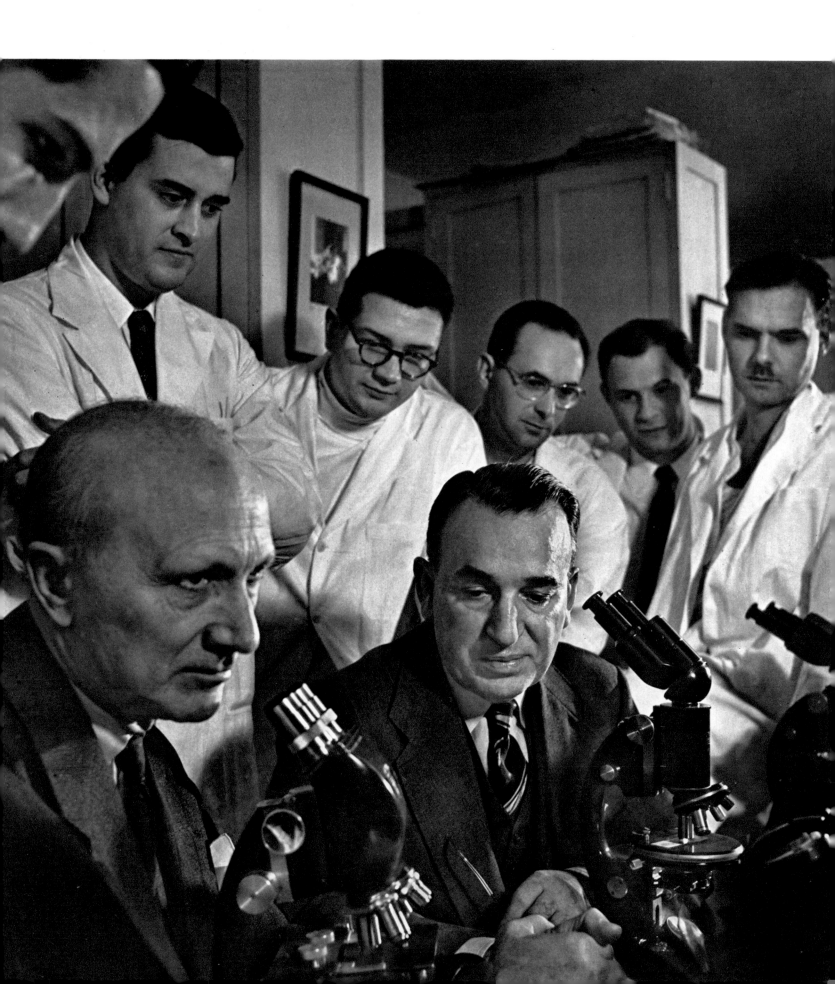

PABLO PICASSO

Pseudonym of Pablo Ruiz; Spanish painter. Born (1881) and educated in Barcelona; a resident of France most of his adult life. Began to work in Paris in 1901; founded and led the Cubist School; designer for Diaghilev Ballet 1917-27; Director of Prado Gallery, Madrid, 1936-9. Among his paintings are: 'Les Arlequins,' 'L'Aveugle,' 'La Famille du singe,' 'Massacre in Korea,' 'War and Peace,' and portraits of Stravinsky, Cocteau, Apollinaire, and Max Jacob. Also noted for his graphics. Now lives near Cannes with his second wife, formerly Mlle Françoise Gillaux, who is also a painter.

'Picasso,' his friends had told me, 'doesn't care.' This, as I found to my sorrow, is quite true. A remarkable artist, who has kept the world of art on tip-toes and in a state of nervous exhaustion for years, he has the rare quality of simply not caring. Especially about appointments. My own experience was different. When I reached his home in time for our arranged appointment in 1954 I found him out, but he had been delayed by the arrival of relatives at the airport. When he arrived, we made a new appointment, at a local gallery where his ceramics were on display. At the gallery I found everybody sceptical about my appointment: they assured me that it would be futile to set up my equipment since Picasso so seldom kept his engagements. However, I stood firm and, to everyone's amazement, the man whose every act is sensational caused yet another sensation by arriving exactly on time. Moreover, he had dressed up for the occasion. His magnificent new shirt made the attendants shake their heads in wonderment; whatever had come over the old lion? ~ A final surprise was in store. Picasso declared that he had seen my work and it interested him greatly. I would have taken this for mere flattery, in atonement for the previous day's delay, if he had not cited many of my portraits which evidently he had remembered. The sitting went smoothly, yet I am sure that such normality on his part was highly abnormal. ~ During a talk about his work, Picasso argued that the true norm of art must vary with every artist. Each had his own laws. For this reason he objected strenuously to the legend of his artistic anarchy. His work was constructive, not destructive. He was a builder, not a destroyer. If people thought differently, that was because they didn't understand what he was trying to do. He was in fact trying to express his vision of reality and if it differed from other men's visions that was because any reality was real only to one man. It differed, for better or worse, in every human mind. Art, he said, began with the individual. Without him, there could be no art. With countless individuals there would be countless versions of art, of reality.

HIS HOLINESS POPE PIUS XII

Born Eugene Pacelli in Rome, 1876; died, 1958. Educated at the Gregorian University and the Roman Seminary. Ordained priest in 1899. Appointed Nuncio in Munich, 1917, and to the Reich, 1920. Made a Cardinal in 1929 and Secretary of State to His Holiness Pope Pius XI, 1930-9; also during these years Archpriest of St. Peter's Basilica. Elected Pope in 1939.

Irrespective of religious doctrine, no one could fail to be profoundly impressed by the personality of His Holiness Pope Pius XII. As I observed him officiating at the magnificent ceremony wherein a saint was canonized at St. Peter's, I saw at once the force of faith which emanated from his frail body, the humanity and intellect that illuminated the ascetic face. I resolved then that a portrait of him must be of the utmost simplicity, with the minimum of background or props. My task was to photograph not the churchman but the human being. ∼ On the day before the sitting I inspected various rooms in the Vatican and chose a background on the assumption that the Pope would be dressed completely in white for his photograph. When, shortly before eight o'clock on a Thursday morning in June 1949, His Holiness glided swiftly into the Throne Room, I was taken aback to find that over his white gown he wore a red, ermine-tipped capella. That patch of colour destroyed all my careful plans. After blessing me, the Pope said he had put aside ten minutes for the photographs. This was the Feast of Corpus Christi and he was to officiate shortly at a first Communion and Confirmation Mass for the children of foreign diplomats. Ten minutes for portraits in colour as well as black and white! ∼ Respectfully I mentioned to His Holiness that I had observed some of his attitudes during the ceremony of canonization and wished to reproduce them. He co-operated most kindly, and though he remained silent throughout the sitting, yet the movement of his translucent, almost opalescent hands, seemed to voice messages. In the heavy silence those eloquent hands fascinated me and I tried to record them with the sensitive face. ∼ Never have I worked so feverishly and with such a sense of urgency. I had visualized this ethereal figure clothed in white. I had hoped to record it surrounded by a group of kneeling children. Now I must improvise everything afresh. As the minutes fled, I almost despaired. The Pope, however, remained a picture of serenity. He seemed to have the power of losing himself entirely in the mood of the moment. Despite my anxiety, the sense of utter peace in this man began to touch my consciousness and give me the sense of another world. To me the Pope's power of communication without a single word was his own special quality. ∼ His Holiness graciously extended the sitting by eight more precious minutes for he realized my difficulties. But I left Vatican City in complete turmoil, thinking of the portraits I could not take, the questions I had not been able to ask. No matter, I came away feeling that those eighteen minutes had been among the most consequential in my life as a portraitist.

THEIR SERENE HIGHNESSES
PRINCE RAINIER III
AND PRINCESS GRACE
OF MONACO

Prince Rainier III is the reigning prince of Monaco, over which the Grimaldi family has ruled since the tenth century. Born 1923; succeeded his grandfather, Prince Louis II, 1949. Educated in England; at Rosey, Switzerland; and at the University of Montpellier, France. Founder of the Red Cross of Monaco, 1948; carried out, on board his yacht, many scientific cruises for the advancement of geographic studies; enlisted with French Army, 1944. After the war he completed his education in Sciences Politiques at the University of Paris. Married, 1956, Miss Grace Kelly, American film actress, whom he met while she was working in a film being made in Monaco. Princess Grace was born in Philadelphia, 1929, and educated at Rainhill convent school; Stevens School, Germantown, Pennsylvania; and the Academy of Dramatic Arts, New York. Broadway début, 1949, in Strindberg's The Father. *Among the films in which she has starred are* High Noon, Rear Window, The Country Girl *(for which she won an award from the Academy of Motion Arts and Sciences, 1954), and* The Bridges at Toko-ri.

To the world public, I judge, Their Serene Highnesses of Monaco represent the latest and most vivid version of Prince Charming and Cinderella. To me they offered a different interest: as subjects for a joint portrait—and excellent subjects too. ∼ This photograph was made in their New York apartment in 1956. The Princess herself took me there ahead of time and together we selected the background for the sitting. The dining room was chosen because it offered a maximum of space. We also inspected the Princess's wardrobe and she obligingly wore the gown I liked best. ∼ Princess Grace's charm and loveliness were not as immediately apparent on the morning of the sitting itself, for she had her hair in pin curls. Unconcerned, however, she went about her business until I asked her to go before my lights. Then, quickly removing the pins, she brushed out her hair with a few strong strokes. I have never seen anything so fresh and alluring. It was like a cool breeze. ∼ The Prince talked freely and, to my surprise, was completely at home in the idiom of American English. The happiness of this couple, who have become the symbol of Romance the world over, was evident. ∼ This portrait shows, I think, the radiant beauty of the woman, the strong, clean-cut profile of the man. It is included in this book because I like it. The Prince and Princess seem to like it also and asked permission to use it as a stamp in their little country . . . the stamp, you might say, of domestic felicity.

NORMAN ROCKWELL

American illustrator; born in New York City, 1894. Left high school in second year to study at the Art Students' League; served as '1st class varnisher and painter' in the United States Navy during World War I. Best known as a painter of magazine covers and illustrations for Saturday Evening Post, Ladies Home Journal, American Magazine, *etc. He has also done murals. Work is represented at Metropolitan Museum, New York.*

Though I am not equipped to say how Norman Rockwell ranks as an artist in the highest sense, I dare say his work is more widely known in America than that of any other painter. He is a superb and painstaking craftsman and he is also a warm enthusiastic human being. ~ He was enthusiastic in 1956 on hearing that I wished to photograph him, and sent a car from Stockbridge, Massachusetts, to fetch me from New York. On reaching his studio, I found a note on the door telling me: 'Please come in and make yourself at home. I will be back at one.' My host arrived shortly afterwards, took me to lunch with some of his friends, and then we got down to work. ~ I wanted to emphasize one of his famous Four Freedom paintings as originally published in the *Saturday Evening Post*, and we chose 'Freedom of Religion' to appear in the background of my portrait. ~ Mr. Rockwell seemed intensely interested in my methods and I soon realized that photography is an essential ingredient of his own art. He told me he employed a regular photographer who, upon his instructions, took pictures of suitable candidates for his paintings. These pictures, blown up to the right size, are pasted over one another or placed in juxtaposition, until the painter has exactly the joint effect he wants—a kind of collective model, I suppose. ~ The characters distilled by his brush follow no particular tradition, he told me, but only 'human interest' and a 'very cheerful realism.' The artist should be an entertainer, not a crusader. For himself, he had very pleasant views on life, which his work reflected. In short, he painted people as he saw them. 'I'm no Goya,' he added. ~ Was art endangered by commercialization? 'It's part of the age,' he replied. 'Everything is commercialized.' There was danger, he admitted, when an artist was pressured into repeating his successful subjects but, he said, 'I do just what I like to do and people seem to like it also. I don't think I'm selling myself down the river.' ~ I asked him if technique could be exalted over integrity. 'Technique,' he retorted, 'is a matter of self-expression. If integrity goes technique alone cannot save it.' ~ This highly popular artist is a profound admirer of more radical painters. He thought Picasso and Matisse among the greatest painters of all time. 'But,' he confessed, 'it's not the kind of thing I like to do. They are expressing something new.' A restless man, Rockwell dashed off one sketch of me after another as I photographed him and threw them all on the floor. There we left them. Unfortunately the likenesses were much too accurate.

RICHARD RODGERS AND OSCAR HAMMERSTEIN

American composer Richard Rodgers was born in New York in 1902; he has composed songs for various musical shows since 1925 including She's My Baby, I Married an Angel, *and* Pal Joey. *American librettist Oscar Hammerstein II was born in New York in 1895; some well-known pre-war shows for which he wrote the words are:* Rose Marie, The Desert Song, Show Boat, New Moon. *Together Rodgers and Hammerstein have written the most extraordinarily successful musicals, for stage and screen, since the days of Gilbert and Sullivan. These include:* Oklahoma, Carousel, Carmen Jones, Allegro, South Pacific, *and* The King and I.

Sometimes two names get so completely married that one can never be thought of without the other. Who ever thinks of Gilbert without Sullivan? Or Rodgers without Hammerstein? In fact Messrs. Rodgers and Hammerstein seem to me almost a reincarnation of Messrs. Gilbert and Sullivan. They bestride the contemporary world of popular music like twin colossi as their predecessors bestrode it in the first days of *Pinafore* and *The Mikado.* ~ I approached the distinguished musical partnership with delight, for the music and lyrics of such shows as *South Pacific* are continually flitting through my mind when I should be thinking of something else. It had been arranged that the two famous collaborators should be photographed, in 1950, at Mr. Rodgers' New York apartment. When I reached it, its owner explained that there would be a slight delay as Mr. Hammerstein had to attend a special rehearsal of the show then in preparation. We spent some pleasant minutes chatting about their work, and, since I am one of their admirers, conversation was easy. I must say, though, that when Mr. Hammerstein arrived I was a little taken aback. How could two such men so utterly different in physical appearance and in bent of mind possibly combine their talents—and without any of those private feuds and public brawls that unhappily disfigured the partnership of Gilbert and Sullivan? ~ The sitting had not been under way long, however, before I realized that two diverse characters complement each other. Their unlikeness fits together perfectly and has produced the complete results that have given so much pleasure throughout the world. ~ But you would not think, at first, to look at them, that these men could write the haunting music now almost their trademark or the lyrics illuminating with wit or a touch of tears the foibles, sometimes the heroism, and always the wistfulness of our time. ~ The harmony of their work together appears, I hope, in their joint portrait—the portrait of a musician and of a writer who do not essay the highest peaks of art, perhaps, but are important artists just the same. They have given to a disordered age a healing melody, in the idiom of their own people, but with a wider appeal that can reach the whole world.

ANNA ELEANOR ROOSEVELT

Born in New York City in 1884; she married Franklin Delano Roosevelt, a distant relative, in 1905; they had one daughter and four sons. Mr. Roosevelt was President of the United States from 1933 to 1945, the year of his death. As America's First Lady for an unprecedented period of twelve years Mrs. Roosevelt exercised enormous influence on public affairs; she has remained active in educational, social, and political affairs and as a leading member of the Democratic party. She was a United States representative to the United Nations General Assembly from 1946 to 1952, and Chairman of the U.N. Committee on Human Rights, 1947-51. She writes extensively on sociological subjects.

If I have little to say about Eleanor Roosevelt it is because the massive contents of her life, and the woman behind them, are too complex a subject for any comment of mine. But I hope this portrait has caught a glimpse of both. ∼ It is one of five portraits (the others being those of Churchill, Eisenhower, Low, and Shaw) which appeared in my earlier book, *Faces of Destiny*. I include Mrs. Roosevelt's portrait here because I like to consider it one of my major successes and because, of course, I have a deep admiration for its subject. ∼ I was attracted at once, like everybody else, by Mrs. Roosevelt's charm, her utter lack of self-consciousness, and that simplicity of manner which has not been altered in the least by her familiarity with the great. She has indeed walked with kings and never lost the common touch. ∼ But what fascinated me most, and seemed somehow to reveal the woman herself, was the shape, the animation, and the eloquence of her hands. I resolved to fix them, if I could, on film, as an essential feature of the portrait. Of course, one could not 'pose' a subject's hands and accomplish anything worthy of this remarkable woman. They must be caught when she was quite unconscious of their gestures. I said nothing, therefore, of my intentions and allowed Mrs. Roosevelt's hands to act out, as it were, their natural part in her personality. Such sensitive and eloquent hands! I watched them as carefully as I watched the face and when their gesture seemed to fit exactly the expression I quickly made the exposure. ∼ Though she was at that time the First Lady of the United States and busy with a thousand things, Mrs. Roosevelt gave me her entire attention and made the sitting one of the easiest, as well as the most delightful, I remember. She did not suspect, however, until she saw the portrait, that her hands were telling me as much as her voice. And I don't suppose that she realizes either that her face, while not conventionally beautiful, has a curious beauty of its own, the reflection of a spacious and dauntless spirit.

ARTUR RUBINSTEIN

Pianist. American of Polish origin; born 1889 and educated at Warsaw and Berlin Academies of Music. A musical prodigy, he gave his first concert in Warsaw in 1895; in 1902 he played with the Berlin Symphony Orchestra. He made his first United States tour in 1906 when he gave 75 concerts in three months. He has toured Europe, South America, Australia, Africa, China, and Japan and has made eight consecutive tours of the United States, Canada, Mexico, and Central America. Many decorations have been awarded him. Lives in California.

One night, around 1.30 A.M., my telephone rang. A great musician had come to Ottawa for a concert and had agreed to have his portrait taken for R.C.A. 'How long will the photograph take?' he inquired. 'Until we are both exhausted,' I replied. ~ Thus began my first encounter with Artur Rubinstein in 1945. When he arrived at my studio next morning I saw that he had made up his mind to be difficult. However, we made a few portraits and I suggested that he return that afternoon. This second session proved calm and peaceful. I said that I would develop his negatives immediately so that he could see proofs before he left the next day. We hardly expected to hear from him until noon at the earliest but at 10 A.M.: 'How are the pictures? I'll come over right away.' I showed him the proofs and then, what a transformation! Until now, he said, he had never liked any of his portraits, had concluded, in fact, that it must be his face he didn't like. Then, looking around the studio walls at the pictures of famous personalities, he addressed them thus: 'Yesterday, I wondered what you had that I hadn't. Now I'm not jealous any more.' ~ During a subsequent photographic session in New York in 1957, Mr. Rubinstein talked a good deal about his art with frank enthusiasm. He told me that before a concert he was tense, nervous, and tired, but afterwards he felt his strength magically renewed. ~ No, he had no thought of retiring . . . ever. He did not intend to make the mistake of retiring to a life of leisure and dying six months later from boredom. Musicians, wrapped up in their art, usually had a long life and his, however long, would be full of work, hence of pleasure. ~ Since Rubinstein is known as a gourmet I asked him if he favoured any particular national cuisine. 'No more than I have a favourite composer. If I had a favourite composer I could not play any of the others. Cooking is an art and must have variety. A concert should be made up like a menu . . . you wouldn't give a guest veal, beef, and chicken in one meal, nor should you give three sonatas in a concert. There must be fish, meat, salad, and dessert.' I thought that this comparison well described Rubinstein himself for, like an impeccable menu, he is a well-rounded personality.

BERTRAND ARTHUR WILLIAM RUSSELL, O.M.

THIRD EARL RUSSELL

British philosopher, mathematician, and educationist. Born 1872 and succeeded his brother to the title in 1931. Educated at Trinity College, Cambridge. Won the Nobel Prize for Literature in 1950. A man of outspoken, unorthodox ideas, of unequalled lucidity in speech and in print. Has been married four times; his fourth marriage, to Edith Finch of New York, occurred in 1952 when he was eighty years old. His works include: A History of Western Philosophy, Human Knowledge: Its Scope and Limits, The Impact of Science upon Society, *and* Why I Am Not a Christian. *In November 1957, he addressed an open letter to President Eisenhower and Mr. Krushchev in the* New Statesman and Nation, *calling on them to put a stop to the continued diffusion of nuclear weapons, and to come to an agreement on the conditions of peaceful co-existence.*

'Happiness,' said the most controversial and certainly the most impish, of modern philosophers, 'comes from pandering to one's self-esteem.' ∼ I judged from the gleam of mischief in Lord Russell's eye that this was likely to prove a controversial sitting. I was wrong. My subject delights to tilt with intellectual giants, he expresses a profound and almost terrifying pessimism, but is quite amenable before the camera. Still, to be with Bertrand Russell is disconcerting. He distracted me with dark thoughts when my mind should have been on my work. Having plied him with provocative questions, to set that wonderful old face in motion, I could not escape the answers. ∼ Since my question about human happiness had received a rather devastating aphorism in reply, I countered with the suggestion that science had given people more leisure which should promote more contentment. 'If,' he said, 'you're talking about the wage-earners, you're quite right; they have more leisure than ever before but others, in all walks of life, probably have less leisure. You have no leisure, I have no leisure.' ∼ The great pessimist was in good form that lovely summer day of 1949 at Llan Festiniog, Wales. I asked what he considered the greatest evil of our times. After a moment's thought, he answered, 'That's hard to tell. But the world has become far, far worse in my time. There's more evil than when I was young. Really, one of the greatest evils these days is the torturing of children to make them betray their parents, as is being done in a very large country and was definitely done in Germany during Hitler's régime.' ∼ Madame Karsh, who accompanied me, thought the sitting had become too sombre in mood; so she asked blithely why there were no great women philosophers. Lord Russell's retort was decisive: 'Lack of personal ambition. Not the singleness of purpose among women to make them willing to give up everything else in the way of human relationship.' ∼ These tart comments on human happiness had produced the sort of revealing expression I desired from my subject. I told him I intended to use his portrait in a companion book to *Faces of Destiny* which would include 'men of peace'—writers, composers, artists, scientists, and philosophers. Lord Russell gave me a wry smile. 'I wish,' he said, 'I could believe that men of that ilk rule our destiny as much as the men of war and state, but I'm very much afraid that it's definitely not so.' We left him chuckling in his cosmic pessimism.

JONAS EDWARD SALK

American medical scientist who perfected world's first effective immunization against poliomyelitis, now known universally as the Salk vaccine. Born in 1914; educated at New York University College of Medicine and College of New York City. New York's Mount Sinai Hospital, 1940-2. Appointments in Epidemiology, University of Michigan, 1943-7. Associate Professor of Bacteriology and Director of Virus Research at University of Pittsburgh's School of Medicine, 1947-9; Research Professor, 1948-54; Professor of Preventive Medicine and Chairman of the Department, 1954-7; Commonwealth Professor of Experimental Medicine since 1957.

The pressure of time gave me no chance to become well acquainted with Dr. Jonas Salk, one of humanity's great benefactors. I faced an early deadline and I had to catch a plane from Pittsburgh, the doctor's home town, to New York. But brief as our meeting was, I retained a definite impression of this relatively young man who bears the firm, clear-eyed face of our scientific age. ∼ Dr. Salk's name is known by now in every corner of the world where his vaccine is conquering polio, but few of those benefiting from his serum can know the labour of six years, sixteen hours a day, six days a week, that went into this discovery. I asked him if he were often requested to make speeches and he admitted that the invitations were numerous—but often had to be declined. 'I decided early in the game,' he remarked, 'to say "no," for it would be too time-consuming. The trouble is that people expect me to pontificate on any subject and to give them an answer to everything. Of course I can't. I'm in the middle of my life and I have work to do. I haven't reached the end of a period.' ∼ What was he working on now? He told me his aim was to evolve single shots of his life-saving vaccine and he pointed suddenly to the syringe in his hand. 'Some day,' he added with a boyish grin, 'I hope we shall be able to inoculate against all known diseases.' A staggering thought, the ultimate hope of medicine and perhaps beyond the reach of any man now alive. But men like Dr. Salk are labouring patiently towards it. He is exploring, indeed, the theory that long-dormant viruses, not yet identified, cause various malignant diseases. If so, a child might be inoculated against them early in life and saved from the maladies of maturity and old age. ∼ Dr. Salk's life is not confined to the laboratory. He told me that one of his most pleasurable experiences had been a conversation with Robert Frost—a conversation put on film to record the views of two great, though dissimilar, men. It was extraordinary, said Dr. Salk, how the hearts and minds of divergent people could so often come into complete accord. ∼ Divergent, yes, but it occurred to me that a scientist such as Salk and a poet such as Frost were really aiming at the same thing—the exploration of life. It was in a mood illustrative of this search that I photographed the scientist, a child before him and on his face the radiant look of a man who has well served children the world over.

CARL SANDBURG

*American poet and biographer; born of Swedish parents in
Illinois, 1878. Sandburg left school at thirteen and did many
odd jobs. Soldiered in Spanish-American War, after which
he worked his way through college, one of his professors paying
for publication of his first volume of poems. Journalist on the
Chicago Daily News; Stockholm correspondent for
Newspaper Enterprise Association, 1918; lecturer at
University of Hawaii, 1934; wrote commentary for United
States Government film Bomber, 1941; weekly columnist
syndicated by the Chicago Times, 1941-5. Awarded Poetry
magazine's Levinson Prize, 1914, and the Pulitzer Prize for
poetry, 1951. For thirty years sought out material on Abraham
Lincoln and produced one of the great biographies in modern
times. Other publications include: Chicago Poems,
Smoke and Steel, Good Morning, America, The
Chicago Race Riots, The People, Yes. Has collected
American folk music and has toured performing this and
reading his own poetry.*

The sitting for this portrait of Carl Sandburg was brief for he could spare
only a few minutes in 1954 in my New York studio-apartment for a portrait,
and less for conversation. Still, the tall, broad figure, the massive, rough-
cast face, the clear eyes, and the mane of white hair falling across the forehead must delight any photographer. One might be photographing a more
than life-size statue carved by a sculptor. ∼ I knew something of the life
which had produced this impressive personage and I deeply admired it.
Sandburg is, and looks, a self-made man. The poverty of his childhood—he
left school at thirteen to help support his family—the years of labour as a
dishwasher, bricklayer, harvester, and jack-of-all-trades are written clearly
on his face and are expressed in his speech. He was blunt to me but friendly.
∼ He placed himself completely at my disposal. 'I'm your puppet,' he said.
He didn't like my electric lights, however. They hurt his eyes. On the street,
he told me, he often wore sun glasses. ∼ I asked the poet what he thought
of the public reading of poetry. 'Nothing much,' he said crisply. 'Few can
deliver it effectively. Some can't read. But some can, and they can even
make bad poetry sound good.' ∼ Then he recalled that I had made a portrait
of Sir Winston Churchill (taken under the same conditions of haste in
Ottawa) which he admired. That gave me the chance to ask Sandburg what
he thought of the British statesman. Were the intelligentsia of London
trying to destroy him? Sandburg laughed at that. 'At one time,' he said, 'I
had a low opinion of Churchill, five or ten years before the war. But he has
grown. All the time he has grown in stature with the people and events.
A great man.' And after a pause he added: 'With the faults of a great man.'

BRIGADIER GENERAL DAVID SARNOFF

American radio and television pioneer and executive. Born in Russia, 1891; educated at New York public school and Pratt Institute. Rose from office boy for Marconi Wireless Telegraph Co. (1906) to Chairman of the Board and Chief Executive Officer of the Radio Corporation of America (1949); Director, National Broadcasting Co. Inc. First to pick up the news that the Titanic was sinking, 1912; he was then operator of the most powerful radio station in New York, on top of John Wanamaker's store. During World War I played important part in equipping United States troops with wireless, and in World War II was General Eisenhower's Communications Consultant. Recipient of many honorary degrees and decorations.

All scientists know that the work of General David Sarnoff, in the field of electronics, has affected every nation in the world. The layman knows that this poor Russian immigrant boy, who became one of America's greatest industrialists, has deeply changed our daily lives by his revolutionary development of radio and television. But what interested me most in this extraordinary man was not his scientific genius or his grasp of big business, but his sense of universal things. ∼ During our talk in his New York skyscraper office in 1956 he told me candidly of his hopes and his fears for the human race which, as he said, had crossed a fateful watershed with the explosion of the first atomic bomb thirteen years ago; he has put kindred thoughts into print. The universe, according to scientists, was at least five billion years old, but General Sarnoff liked to think that our world is about thirteen years 'young.' For a new life, or its possibility, had been born with man's mastery of the atom. The power thus placed in man's hands, he said, was so great—almost beyond our imagination—that we dare not fumble. But technical knowledge, expanding by leaps and bounds every day, was not enough if the new power was to serve, instead of destroy, our species. ∼ Most of all, he added earnestly, man needs time for contemplation of those individual forces represented by the mysterious qualities of the atom. Science had given us wonderful tools to be used in creating the long-sought Brotherhood of Man on earth, 'but the mortar of Brotherhood does not come from any laboratory. It must come from the heart and mind.' ∼ As more secrets were wrested from nature, he said, the logic and rhythm of life took on more meaning. But for all his cunning, man was not equipped to understand the order of the universe by reason; yet by an intuition, far beyond reason, he could see therein the clear manifestations of a Divine Intelligence and Supreme Architect of the Universe. Thus science, for Sarnoff, provided no substitute for religious teaching and moral precepts. Indeed these spiritual sheet anchors were more necessary than ever when mankind was spinning through a completely new experience across an unmapped terrain. ∼ Through his window General Sarnoff looked out that morning of our sitting upon the concrete canyons of New York. But he was looking far beyond these monuments to man's material achievements. Then, turning back to me with an expression of peculiar radiance, he put his conclusion into words. 'Material progress,' he said, 'is a delusion unless it is put at the service of eternal spiritual value.'

ALBERT SCHWEITZER

French missionary-surgeon, founder of Hospital at Lambaréné,
French Equatorial Africa (1913). Born 1875 in Upper Alsace;
educated at Universities of Strasbourg, Paris, and Berlin;
obtained degrees in philosophy, theology, and medicine.
Organist, J. S. Bach Society, Paris, 1903-11, and an expert on
Bach's music. Awarded Nobel Peace Prize in 1952. Has
written many books, on his work in Africa, on Bach, and on
religious subjects. Holds many honorary degrees.

It had taken me a long time to meet 'le Grand Docteur.' For several years I had wondered how I should ever reach his home and hospital in Lambaréné, French Equatorial Africa, but then by good luck, I found myself in France in 1954 when he happened to visit his home town, Gunsbach, in Alsace. ~ When one has read all Dr. Schweitzer's works and long admired him from the distance, one fears that the actual man may fall below the imagined image. But he is all that one imagines he will be. I felt at once, as all men do, the presence of a conscious and immense wisdom, the stronger for its utter simplicity. ~ Of course, he said, my wife and I and my assistant must have lunch with him, and it was a luncheon frugal in the extreme. But after luncheon we were served with excellent coffee and I began then to get a glimpse of a universal mind which still has time for the smallest human detail. This coffee, he explained, was made from beans five years old. 'Coffee made from young beans is toxic. After the beans are about five years old they are medicinal, in fact beneficial.' ~ What struck me from the beginning was this man's power to concentrate his mind totally on the business at hand. While the equipment was being prepared he went back to his writing as if he were alone in the room and then, when I was ready, he gave me his full attention. ~ Of course a thousand questions were on my tongue and it was tantalizing to realize that I would not have time to ask a fraction of them. While we talked I watched Dr. Schweitzer closely, especially his hands. They were the fine hands of a musician and a healer. I wished to photograph him holding some books, preferably an album of Bach, but he protested that to use Bach's music for this purpose would be like 'choucroute garnie.' Accordingly, with a shy smile, he brought out some of his own books. And then he revealed a very human side, by declining to be photographed while wearing his spectacles. 'They make me look too old,' he said. ~ It was, of course, my hope not so much to make the portrait that Schweitzer might desire, but to catch him, if possible, at an unconscious moment when perhaps my camera might seize something of those qualities which have made him great as a doctor, musician, philosopher, humanitarian, theologian, and writer. The picture printed here was taken in a moment of meditation. ~ Remembering his tolerance, and his ministrations to the African natives, I asked him how he thought Christ would be received if He were to appear in our time. Dr. Schweitzer looked up at me and in his quiet voice replied, 'People would not understand Him at all.' Which, then, did he consider the most important of the Ten Commandments? He thought about that for a long moment, the granite face was illuminated, the man behind the legend suddenly visible. 'Christ,' he said, 'gave only one Commandment. And that was Love.'

GEORGE BERNARD SHAW

Irish playwright, novelist, critic, and philosopher; one of the founders of the Fabian Society, 1884. Born in Dublin, 1856; died at Ayot St. Lawrence, England, 1950. Educated at Wesley College, Dublin, and received some training in music and painting at home. Went to London, 1876. Began to come into prominence in 1885 as music critic (writing under the pseudonym Corno di Bassetto for the Star *and later the* World), *drama critic, book-reviewer, and propagandist for socialism. Awarded the Nobel Prize for Literature, 1925. His published works include some fifty plays and many novels, essays, treatises, etc. Best known among these are perhaps the plays* St. Joan, Major Barbara, Pygmalion, Arms and the Man, The Doctor's Dilemma, *and* Heartbreak House, *and the essays* The Perfect Wagnerite *and* The Intelligent Woman's Guide to Socialism.

Though this portrait appeared in my earlier book, I include it here for two reasons: no collection which includes modern thinkers would be complete without G.B.S.; and I happen to like my photograph of him. Happily Shaw shared that opinion. ∼ I'm glad he liked it but I must say every obstacle was in my way when I first met him in 1943. To begin with, his secretary laid down drastic and quite impossible terms. I was to have five minutes only with the great man. There were to be no lights. I could use nothing but a 'miniature camera.' While I was arguing vainly Shaw himself came bursting into the room with the energy of a young man, though he was then almost ninety years old. His manner, his penetrating old eyes, his bristling beard, and crisp speech were all designed to awe me and, in the beginning, they succeeded. Shaw said he could see no reason why I should photograph him anyway. I explained that the Government of Canada wished to have a good portrait of him in the National Archives at Ottawa. 'Since when,' he retorted, 'does the Canadian Government know a good picture when it sees one? And in any case why did they not commission Augustus John at a thousand guineas and make sure of the job? If John did it, the job would be good—or at any rate everybody would think so.' Plucking up my courage, I suggested that perhaps I had been assigned to make the portrait for that same reason. ∼ In the end I had all the time I wanted and I think Shaw enjoyed himself. For he was a better actor than many who appeared in his plays and he obviously loved to act. His favourite role seemed to be that of a sort of harmless Mephistopheles, or the grumpy wicked uncle with a heart of gold. After he had tested me with preliminary terror we got along beautifully. ∼ He said I might make a good picture of him, but none as good as the picture he had seen at a recent dinner party. There he had glimpsed, over the shoulder of his hostess, what he took to be a perfect portrait of himself—cruel, you understand, a diabolical caricature but absolutely true. He had pushed by the lady, approached that living image, and found that he was looking into a mirror! The old man peered at me quizzically to see if I appreciated his little joke. It was then that I caught him in my portrait. ∼ Later on, a noted British journalist asked me to prepare a copy of this picture which he proposed to have autographed by Shaw. To his chagrin, he received the picture with Shaw's signature scrawled on the back of it. When asked for an explanation Shaw replied: 'I was careful to make sure that my signature should not distract from my face.' Nothing could, I think, distract from that face.

JEAN JULIUS SIBELIUS

Finnish composer (1865–1957). Educated at Helsinki University and at Berlin and Vienna Conservatories. In 1897 Finland gave him a life grant on which he was able to retire and devote himself to creative work. His music is profoundly individual, national, and poetic in character. His works, among the best known of which are Finlandia *and* The Swan of Tuonela, *include seven symphonies, a violin concerto, about two hundred compositions for piano and over a hundred songs. Held many honorary degrees.*

One day when I was photographing an official of Shell Oil, London, the telephone rang. 'Helsinki on the line,' a secretary said. The official apologized for the interruption. 'On the contrary,' I said, 'Helsinki has a magic sound in my ear.' I told him of my long but thwarted ambition to photograph Sibelius. Wires were soon humming, both telephonic and telegraphic, between the British and Finnish capitals and soon afterwards I found myself on the threshold of a simple house in Jarvenpaa, near Helsinki, a house built for Sibelius by a grateful nation, a shrine for all lovers of music. ~ The man who ushered me into his home in 1949 was well into his eighties, and near the end of his life. His hands shook but his mind was wonderfully alert, and he told me that he followed the news of the world in careful detail. ~ We spent a leisurely day of photography punctuated, at intervals, with a break for coffee, cakes, and brandy. Sibelius would call for a toast and then raise an empty glass. 'You see,' he explained, 'I never drink before dinner.' He seemed to be a happy man full of infectious laughter. His little jokes were uttered in French, since I had no Finnish and he little English, but sometimes, stuck for a word, he appealed to one of his daughters, who translated for him. ~ Towards the end of the day when Sibelius appeared fatigued I told him a little story. During the Russo-Finnish war, I said, there were many Finns cutting timber in the Canadian North and, hearing the dire news from home, they brooded and slackened in their work. Production in the camps began to drop. The foreman, with sudden inspiration, acquired a recording of *Finlandia* and piped it to the loggers in the woods. Immediately, the output of timber doubled. Sibelius rocked with mirth. 'You're fantastic!' he cried, 'one never gets tired working with you.' ~ I was not satisfied with that day's work, however, and suggested another sitting. He agreed, and I returned next morning when the portrait printed here was made. ~ Before leaving I presented him with various gifts entrusted to me by some of his admirers in England. As Sibelius said, with another chuckle, these introductory offerings should have been made at the first, not the last moment. He accepted them all with delight. ~ When he said good-bye a barefoot, tow-headed boy of five years appeared from nowhere, the composer's great-grandson, and stood before the old man with his hands clasped as if in worship. The sun poured over the profile of these two, the very young and the very old, destiny yet ahead and destiny fulfilled. Nothing could have done justice to the flaxen hair of the child, to the gentleness of the aged man. Some pictures are better left in memory alone.

IGOR SIKORSKY

American aircraft designer. Born in Russia, 1889; educated at the Naval College, St. Petersburg, and the Institute of Technology, Kiev. Head engineer, aviation factory, Russo-Baltic Railroad Car Works, 1912-18; built and flew first multi-motored plane, 1913; designed and built four-motored bombers for Russian Army. Arrived in United States, 1919; developed many types of aircraft, including Sikorsky amphibian and Sikorsky helicopter (the only helicopters used by the American Air Forces during World War II). Associated with several aircraft corporations; retired in 1957 from Sikorsky Aircraft Division of United Aircraft Corporation. Holds many honorary degrees and awards from United States and abroad.

As we chatted in his office at Bridgeport, Connecticut, in 1957, Sikorsky looked up suddenly from the blueprints on his desk—looked up at the ceiling actually, but he seemed to be looking towards the sky, the scene of his lifework, the focus of his dreams. Thus I photographed him and I think the symbolism of this portrait is accurate. ~ Sikorsky has a powerful and altogether Russian face, the face of a dreamer and a man of action too. His voice is soft yet firm with still more than a trace of Russian accent. I found him easy in conversation, unwilling to take the slightest credit that he felt was not rightly his. ~ When I said that I always considered him 'the father of the helicopter,' he denied the title at once. True enough, he had experimented with the idea of the helicopter at the age of only nineteen years, but the first workable machine had been flown in 1937 by a German, H. Focke, not by him. However, he was proud to be able to say that he had been the first to design, construct, and fly a multiple-engine (four) aircraft as well as the first successful helicopter in the Western hemisphere. ~ I wondered what might be expected from flight, which is rapidly revolutionizing our planet and perhaps reaching out towards others. For example, would the time come when aircraft, and especially helicopters, would be as generally used as is the automobile today? No, he said emphatically, this could not happen. It was absurd to compare the automobile on the two-dimensional highway with a machine travelling through the vast three-dimensional 'ocean of air.' Flying would always present problems demanding of the aviator a firm knowledge of air currents, wind velocity, altitude, astronomy, and all sciences related to air travel. Just as few people had the capacity to navigate a ship on the high seas, so few had the temperament to become air pilots. Ingenuously I asked him whether his early thinking about helicopters had been influenced by the humming-bird which can move upward or downward or hover in the air. Sikorsky was sorry to spoil my little fancy, but he had not been thinking of humming-birds. The principle of the helicopter he said, was very ancient and had been conceived by Leonardo da Vinci. ~ He spoke with a surprising tenderness of his S-42, the first American Clipper which, after many flights from North to South America, was presented to the Ford Museum at Dearborn. He had delivered it to the museum himself and, he recalled, with a glint in his eye, it was still a 'living plane.' Most relics in museums were only shells, but the Clipper contained all its original parts and reached its last refuge under its own power.

JOHN ERNST STEINBECK

*American novelist of German and Northern Irish descent;
born in California in 1902. Educated at Stanford University.
Much of his work is a reflection of his native district, the
Californian interior valleys and the Monterey coast; has a
thorough knowledge of marine biology. Tried his hands at
many jobs; he made his name in literature with* Grapes of
Wrath, *which won the 1939 Pulitzer Prize. Other books
include:* Tortilla Flat, Of Mice and Men, Cannery
Row, The Moon is Down, East of Eden, *and* The
Short Reign of Pippin IV. *In 1943, he went to Europe as
correspondent for the New York* Herald Tribune. *Since
World War II, he has travelled extensively, writing articles
and reports for various magazines and newspapers.*

The American author who writes of exceedingly earthy characters maintained in Paris a very elegant address. The gate was opened for me, in 1954,
by a butler in black coat and striped trousers. ~ There were, however,
difficulties in this impressive setting. Sunshine poured into the room, cur-
tains had to be changed, and the electricity supply, as usual in the eccentric
power system of France, proved insufficient. Moreover, a continuous
stream of people poured through the room—the author's wife, his children
one after the other, and his secretary. When the procession was interrupted
for a moment I seized the chance, abandoned the French current, and took
this portrait with electronic lights. ~ Mr. Steinbeck had talked little during
the sitting. His mind was on his own business and on the many urgent
questions brought by his secretary. It seemed that a craftsman skilled in
revealing the character of other people guarded himself jealously from
prying eyes—that here was a courteous but reticent man who did not wear
his heart on his sleeve. However, over refreshments served on the terrace,
he thawed somewhat and volunteered an amusing little story to prove, as
he said, how difficult it sometimes is to be the wife of a celebrity. Mr. and
Mrs. Steinbeck, it appeared, had been entertained recently at a large reception of some sort when Zsa Zsa Gabor, the impetuous movie star from
Hungary and Hollywood, arrived in her usual flutter. She caught sight of
Mr. Steinbeck and rushed at him, oozing charm. 'But John,' she purred,
'you are the one man I have wanted to meet for, oh so long!' Then she
launched into what Steinbeck called 'a very intimate conversation,' ignoring everyone else around her. Finally, Mrs. Steinbeck could endure this
invasion no longer. She thrust herself between Steinbeck and Gabor and
announced, in a cold voice: 'Miss Gabor, I am Mrs. Steinbeck.' That,
apparently, ended that. At the recollection, Steinbeck permitted himself
a rumble of laughter. I saw in him then for the first time, a long way from
his home, some of the qualities of the life in his books.

IGOR STRAVINSKY

Russian-born composer who has been an American citizen since 1945. Born St. Petersburg 1882; studied law at St. Petersburg University and music under Rimski-Korsakov. Naturalized French subject in 1934. Compositions include: L'Oiseau de feu, Petrouchka, Le Sacre du printemps, Orpheus, several symphonies and concertos, and ballet music.

It has been said by his good friend Aldous Huxley that Igor Stravinsky is one of those happy intellectual amphibians who seem to be at home on the dry land of words or in the ocean of music. So I found him. But his words were not dry, if that word means dull. On the contrary, speaking in a free mixture of English and French, he entertained my wife and myself in California, in 1956, with a one-man symphony of conversation, witty and wise. ∼ Before getting down to work, he said, we must have refreshment and relaxation. Whether working or relaxed, Stravinsky does not exhibit any of the so-called artistic temperament. However, he did restrict the rooms which could be used for photography. Indeed, the space at my disposal was so small that I said I hoped in the next world I would enjoy a little more elbow room. To which he replied: 'Not only you, Mr. Karsh!' ∼ Like some of the other composers I have photographed, Stravinsky complained that orchestra conductors in general never asked composers how their work should be played. They believed they knew better than the men who wrote it the proper method of rendition. Yet most conductors didn't understand eighteenth-century music at all. They thought even Bach should be played in a romantic style which was never his intention. ∼ Then Stravinsky took off, with acidulous eloquence, about music critics. Few of them, he said, were really qualified musicians, but they had successfully created a cult of the conductor, regardless of merit. As a result, many conductors had become little more than showmen. 'It's easier, you know,' he remarked, 'to become a critic of writing or painting than of music. Everyone can read or look at a painting but few of the music critics can read music properly.' ∼ He talked at length about music recordings which, he admitted, had improved greatly in a mechanical sense. But that did not necessarily mean improved music. Some of the older records were by far the best musically.' ∼ Stravinsky is one of the few creative artists of my acquaintance who shows a deep interest in his wife's work. Madame Stravinsky, a painter of talent, was unfortunately absent at the moment but Stravinsky observed, with obvious pride, that she was attending an exhibition of her work at Santa Barbara. ∼ He has a strong admiration also for the artists of the written word. In his little library he showed me some photographs of Tolstoi, Verlaine, T. S. Eliot, Aldous and Julian Huxley, and Virginia Woolf, among others. ∼ I also discovered that he admires and is a connoisseur of tobacco. Wherever he goes, he told me, he carries his own cigarettes, made by an Armenian in the United States, of Turkish tobacco and English paper. ∼ In everything, I thought, this man is a perfectionist, especially in his work. When I expressed my own pleasure in it he quoted from Oscar Wilde in French: 'Un homme n'est vraiment intelligent que par son travail.'

FRANCIS HENRY TAYLOR

American museum director (1903-1957). Educated at the Universities of Pennsylvania, Paris, and Florence; Institut d'Estudis Catalans, Barcelona; American Academy, Rome. With Philadelphia Museum of Art as Assistant Curator (1927-8) and Curator of Medieval Art (1928-31); Director of Worcester (Mass.) Art Museum, 1931-40; Director of the Metropolitan Museum of Art, New York, 1940-55 (Director Emeritus, Special Consultant, and Trustee, 1955-7); Director of the Worcester Art Museum, 1955-7. Chairman of the Advisory Committee, Walters Art Gallery, Baltimore, 1934-44; Regional Director for New England States, Federal Art Projects, 1933-4; member of the Advisory Committee on Art, United States Department of State, lecturing in leading South American art museums; member of the American Commission for Protection and Salvage of Artistic and Historic Monuments in War Areas, 1943-6.

To think of Francis Henry Taylor is to remember his dark eyes so luminous with intelligence and that strong Florentine nose, the nose of a man eager, inquisitive, and determined. He was that rare blend of enthusiast and critic. Art was his life and to the collection, appreciation, and preservation of great works of art, he devoted his energy and discrimination. ~ This picture was taken at the end of July 1957, about four months before he died. I think it was appropriate that it was taken in the great hall of the Worcester Art Museum, which was opened in 1933 shortly after Taylor first went there as director. This hall was a favourite place of his, where he liked to stand and reflect. It held the famous mosaics from Antioch and the exquisite tapestry of the Last Judgment, both of them acquisitions which he was proud to have made for Worcester. ~ My memories of Taylor are vivid, for he was a vivid, crisp, and outspoken person. Sometimes, he confessed, he wondered what art was coming to in the days of abstract painting. Thus he could find no admiration for Picasso, whom he called 'Le Gigolo de la Peinture.' When Taylor had once attended an exhibition of Picasso's work he had remarked, out of politeness, that it was wonderful what the painter had found. To which Picasso replied: 'Je ne trouve pas. Je découvre.' Next thing we knew, Taylor told me, Picasso would be walking on water. When Augustus John was painting Taylor's portrait the two men apparently agreed on modern art. 'Abstract painting,' said John, 'won't go on. It's not amusing enough.' ~ Anyway, Taylor insisted that the art of all ages should be judged by the same high standards. 'We can't have a double standard,' he once said, 'a gold standard reserved for the Old Masters and a blocked currency standard for a national art of the present.' ~ He was glad to be out of New York. 'To stay there one has to be either very young or very rich. I've passed the time of the first and I will never achieve the second.' ~ New England beckoned to him as a sanctuary for reflection, for writing, for the renewal of his study of art after the unsparing attrition of his administrative duties. At the time I photographed him, he was in the midst of giving a course at the Harvard Summer School on 'The Growth of Public and Private Taste,' and in these lectures he was really making a road map of the big book he had been looking forward to writing, the sequel to his first great history of collecting *The Taste of Angels*. His mind was full and eager with this great project, but alas, his time of peace and reflection was to be very brief.

ARNOLD JOSEPH TOYNBEE, C.H.

British historian; born 1889. Educated at Winchester and Balliol College, Oxford. Director of Studies, Royal Institute of International Affairs, and Research Professor of International History in the University of London, 1925-55; Professor Emeritus, 1955. Director, Research Department, Foreign Office, 1943-6. His magnum opus *is* A Study of History *whose tenth and final volume was published in 1954. The work considers the causes of the rise and fall of earlier civilizations and of the chief societies or civilizations in existence today, including the Western, the Orthodox Christian, the Syriac, the Hindu, and the Far Eastern.*

I entered the impressive portals of the Royal Institute of International Affairs, in 1955, with a sense of occasion and not a little apprehension. For I was to photograph there the Institute's renowned Director of Studies and perhaps the most remarkable, or at least the most controversial, historian of modern times. But I found in Professor Arnold Toynbee not the chilly scholar of civilizations, as I had expected, but a laughing philosopher. ∼ He greeted me at first with urbane courtesy as if I were the ambassador of some great power or a fellow student of the ages. Of course, if I wished it, the portrait must be made in some other office, for his, as I diffidently intimated, was too small and, as one would expect, cluttered with shelves, books, and furniture. Accordingly he asked his secretary to show me over the whole building so that I could find a suitable background. Alas, as so often is the case in the great institutions of learning, the rooms, with their masses of volumes and papers, the tools of scholarship, were all occupied. In the end I selected a completely empty and impersonal chamber which, if it did not add to the Professor's personality, could not detract from it. When he entered and the sitting began, I realized that I need not have worried about background and *décor*. Toynbee's personality is so effervescent and compelling that it stands out against and quite obliterates the background. ∼ He talked with extraordinary animation about the affairs of mankind, ancient and modern. But the historian who has charted the rise and fall of civilizations, the rhythmical record of aeons, preferred, in talking, to amuse me with a series of light jests, almost as if I were the subject and he the portraitist. His mind moved with lightning speed and so did his mobile features. Too fast, in fact. For whenever he launched on some anecdote, the humour of it touched him prematurely and he would burst into laughter long before the point was reached. He was after all, I reflected, a historian, not an actor. ∼ Yet people always tell me, on seeing this photograph, that this carefree person cannot be the solemn author of that profound and shattering work *A Study of History*. Actually, the portrait seems to me extremely accurate. It shows a man who knows the record of human life as few men know it and, with all its faults, crimes, and tragedies, finds it hopeful, good . . . and laughable.

RALPH VAUGHAN WILLIAMS, O.M.

British composer (1872-1958). Educated at Charterhouse and Trinity College, Cambridge. Studied music at London's Royal College of Music, Berlin, and Paris. Vigorously revived and used in his symphonic works much English folk music. Was largely responsible for the amazing development of public appreciation for indigenous British music. Works include: Sea Symphony, London Symphony, Hugh the Drover, Sixth Symphony, Eighth Symphony, The Pilgrim's Progress.

It was my great pleasure to have had an opportunity to photograph this eminent British composer, who died in 1958. He had been somewhat reluctant to be photographed, but this reluctance quickly disappeared in the first few minutes of our meeting in Dorking, England, in 1949. He proved to be courtesy and co-operation personified—a man of imposing serenity. We chatted freely about a joint enthusiasm. ～ I asked him why the works of Mozart alone appeared to please both the expert and the layman? And why was it that tuneful, graceful music of Mozart's type was no longer composed? 'The reason is,' he said, 'that there has been only one Mozart, and there is certainly none like him today.' ～ The great mathematicians, I remarked, were often good musicians. Did this phenomenon work the other way around? 'Definitely not,' Vaughan Williams chuckled. 'But I wish it did. Why, I can hardly add two and two.' ～ I was interested to know what he thought of the public's musical taste. Had it improved in his lifetime? 'Yes, it has,' he replied. 'But radio, as a conveyer of music, has had a dual effect, a good one and a bad one. More people listen to music these days than ever before, of course, but fewer ever play an instrument.' ～ What place would he regard as the most influential in the world of music? 'London, without doubt,' he said. 'Provided the composer is a foreigner, London is the city which now decides the fate of a new composition. In New York there is so much enthusiasm that almost anything goes.' ～ Many composers, I remarked, resented the fact that they were not consulted by a conductor as to how their work should be played. Vaughan Williams apparently felt differently. 'I have no objection or antagonistic feeling,' he said, 'when people tell me how they interpret my music. I can only reply that I write music and it is there for people to interpret as they wish. Flowers produce different scents which, when blended, produce a perfume that has its own independent existence.' ～ When I completed my portraits, the composer entrusted me with an autographed copy of one of his own symphonies. I was to take and present it to the great Sibelius in Finland. ～ The big, shaggy-haired Englishman escorted me to his gate and called after me: 'Come back anytime—come back soon.'

BRUNO WALTER

Conductor. Born in Germany (1876), where he studied at the Stern Conservatory of Music, Berlin. Musical Director at Munich and Berlin Operas in succession. Fled from Hitler's persecution to Paris and became a French citizen in 1938; again escaped Nazi Germany by going to the United States when France was occupied; he became an American citizen in 1946. Guest conductor at Covent Garden Opera, London; Metropolitan Opera, New York; Salzburg and Edinburgh Music Festivals; and of the New York Philharmonic and other orchestras throughout the United States and Europe.

When I met him for the first time, in 1956, Bruno Walter was recording *Mozart's Requiem* in a New York studio. He seemed to me—and further acquaintance confirmed that original impression—one of the gentlest and most sensitive conductors I had ever encountered. ~ His face, full of tenderness, suffering, and understanding, lit up with indescribable delight as the music welled out of his orchestra; then an infinite melancholy suffused his features, and finally a look of irritation. Something had evidently gone wrong. ~ The disc was played back to him and all the musicians in the studio looked enraptured. They thought the recording perfect. But Dr. Walter dressed in what I call his 'High Priest's' garment, his arms folded, listened with a stern, rather sceptical expression. He picked up his baton and rapped the rostrum. 'Once again, gentlemen, please!' he said tersely. The entire recording was repeated. This time he was satisfied. 'It's wonderful, isn't it, maestro?' the tenor whispered. 'Yes,' said Dr. Walter, 'this time you sang the right C.' I realized then that, with all his sensitivity, this man had necessarily an unyielding firmness, an artistic integrity which would brook no compromises, no second-best. I greatly desired to add such an artist to my portrait collection. ~ He arrived at my New York studio-apartment dressed in a business suit rather than his robes of office as I expected. I felt that our moods were thus not in harmony, and was doubtful of success, for a good sitting is the result of an infinite subtlety of reactions between photographer and subject. Bruno Walter must have divined my feeling for he volunteered another sitting at his home in Beverly Hills. There, on his own ground, in his own environment, and in the ascetic yet characteristic garb of his home and rehearsals, I photographed him.

PAUL DUDLEY WHITE

American physician. Born 1886; educated at Harvard University. On staff of Massachusetts General Hospital since 1911; Teaching Fellow and later Professor of Clinical Medicine, Harvard University, 1914-56; engaged in research and practice and teaching of medicine, specializing in heart diseases. One of founders of American Heart Association, 1922; author of standard reference work on Heart Disease. *Received Lasker Award for distinguished achievement in the field of cardiovascular diseases. Chairman, American Medical Teaching Mission to Greece, Italy, Pakistan, India, Israel.*

My talk with Dr. White, as I photographed him in 1957 in his office in Boston, was highly scientific; or so it appeared to a layman. But doubtless to this slight, small man with a rare twinkle in his eye, my questions were elementary. He answered them readily, simply, and cheerfully. Patience, I suspect, must be the secret of his distinguished career as an investigator of that wonderful machine, the human heart. ∼ The first book I noticed on the table of his waiting room was one called *Low Fat Diets* and it immediately reminded me of Stefansson's theory of a high-fat diet as practised in the Arctic. Dr. White admitted, with a laugh, that he had been exchanging dietary opinions with the great explorer. This was typical of Dr. White. He is eager for information from every source. But, as a matter of fact, he said, in heart or other diseases the amount of fat necessary in a diet depended solely on the individual. ∼ He does insist that heredity plays a larger part in any person's health than is generally supposed. He told me that many people could be saved from premature death or crippling diseases if their doctors knew more of their family histories. If people who write the names of their relatives in family Bibles would include a few words about their illnesses, operations, and general health, a physician, with such a family history, would have an invaluable guide in treating the young. ∼ We were now launched on a subject fascinating to a layman. What, I asked, about the causes of hypertension from which everybody seems to suffer more or less? Did it come from stress? No, it was mainly caused by heredity, the doctor replied; stress only aggravated it. He agreed, however, that the pace of modern living was an unfortunate factor in diseases of the nervous system. Finally, he gave me a useful piece of advice—constant exercise at all times of life, including old age. He especially approved of walking, his own favourite exercise, the natural exercise of man. Or cycling: he has been trying to arrange for the construction of bicycle paths in his neighbourhood in the hope (optimistic, I thought) that people would pedal to work. ∼ His own habits had clearly made Dr. White in his old age a perfectly healthy man, and a happy one. But he put it all down to his family medical history, remarking with a chuckle: 'Mine is a pure case of heredity. My father was a family doctor.'

THORNTON WILDER

American novelist and dramatist; born 1897. When nine years old went to China, where father was Consul-General at Hong Kong and Shanghai; graduated at Yale and studied at American Academy in Rome. Taught in New Jersey, 1921-8; lecturer at University of Chicago, 1930-6. His first novel, The Cabala, *was published in 1926 and the same year his first play,* The Trumpet Shall Sound, *was staged.* The Bridge of San Luis Rey *in 1927 received the Pulitzer Prize; he also won Pulitzer Prizes for his plays* Our Town *and* The Skin of Our Teeth. *Other plays include* The Matchmaker *and* A Life in the Sun. *Served in A.A.F. 1942-5. Awarded Legion of Merit, M.B.E., Chevalier de la Légion d'Honneur.*

As I opened the door of my New York studio in May 1956, I was delighted to find a man with bushy eyebrows (nature's gift to portraitists) and, beneath them, eyes of dancing, sparkling animation. Thornton Wilder won me over at first sight. ~ The American novelist and playwright is a refreshing man, not only in his work but in his conversation. He carried our sitting along in a flow of lively anecdote and raillery. But he turned serious when I told him that I was worried about finding a title for this book, as I felt the wrong sort of title would do a great deal of harm. ~ At once, as if we were old friends, Wilder tried to invent the proper title but was not satisfied with any of his own suggestions. Finally he consoled me with this thought: 'Play or book, the wrong title may be injurious for the first year or so but in the long run it doesn't matter. The content of the book will carry it along.' ~ He went on to recall his recent speaking tour of German universities which evidently had interested him greatly. 'After their experiences of war and American occupation,' he said, 'the youth of German universities has a somewhat sadistic hope that the American speaker will make a fool of himself, one way or another. Yet it's characteristic of the German nation as a whole that it wants the answer to its problems and hopes the speaker will be able to provide it. Of course, he can't. I began by disappointing them, I suppose, but then little by little I ventured to give them some thoughts. They didn't amount to much though. No one can give the answer to anybody else.' ~ At this, my assistant, who had literary ambitions, felt he must ask: 'Mr. Wilder, what advice would you give to a young writer?' Wilder's eyebrows seemed to grow bushier and the eyes took on extra sparkle. He looked hard at the youth and replied: 'Sit down at a desk and write!' ~ Then his serious mood gave way to lighter thoughts. 'Chores, chores, chores,' he complained with comical dismay. 'So many absurd things I have to do when I come to New York when all I want to do is to play and enjoy the most wonderful city in the world!'

TENNESSEE WILLIAMS

American playwright. Born 1912; educated at Universities of Missouri, Iowa, and Washington (St. Louis). Awarded a Rockefeller Fellowship in 1940 for playwriting; in 1943 received a $1,000 grant from the National Institute of Arts and Letters and won Pulitzer Prizes in 1948 and 1955. His plays include: The Glass Menagerie, A Streetcar Named Desire, Summer and Smoke, The Rose Tattoo, Cat on a Hot Tin Roof; *he has also written many successful film plays.*

Tennessee Williams' reply to my desire to photograph him was enthusiastic and spontaneous, like his plays. We met in his small New York apartment in 1956 and decided that the portrait should be made in his own environment, and I came to realize that this jovial, homespun man contained a tumultuous talent and a soul seldom at peace. ∼ Superficially, the plot for this sitting—a sort of minor play rather on the comic side, with Mr. Williams as the comedian and the photographer as his foil—was quite perfect. I had found the master in the scene of his work, surrounded by his typewriter, his manuscript, and his ever present glass of Scotch. Moreover, he seemed to be surrounded by invisible friends. His telephone was constantly ringing as if for the deliberate purpose of distracting me. ∼ His obvious desire to co-operate with me and the feigned calm I can sometimes command in a pinch enabled us, however, to deal with invisible friends—and some visible ones—and to get on with the portrait. ∼ I asked him whom he considered the greatest American actress. He mentioned no woman born in America but remarked that Anna Magnani, the Italian, had acted in American movies and therefore might be technically within my definition. And he left no doubt that he considered her the greatest living member of her profession. It was for her, he said, that he had specially written *The Rose Tattoo.* ∼ At the moment he was working on *Orpheus Descending,* which had been a failure on its first presentation. 'It was performed,' he told me, 'only once, before a Boston audience, and the critics decided it should expire —and it did.' He was therefore rewriting it. ∼ At last the portrait was done and when I showed it to some of my friends they remarked that it looked exactly like Williams' plays. Perhaps. At any rate, the playwright's deceptive ease of manner, his informal speech, and carefree air reminded me of various characters made by his pen—ordinary-looking men hiding an unsuspected fury which invariably erupts on the stage, often in tragedy. ∼ As Mr. Williams admitted rather shyly to me, and as he has written in moments of candour, he is a man burning with a sense of life and desperate to communicate it somehow to his fellows. He cannot communicate it freely in conversation because, he says, there is a certain sense of social restraint even among friends meeting face to face; to the great, dark, faceless audience of the theatre he can at last speak freely without any reticence. ∼ The public knows with what power and sometimes with what nobility he can thus speak. I hope this portrait catches at least a spark of that volcanic inward fire which makes each of his plays a sort of spiritual convulsion and leaves the audience limp with spent emotion.

FRANK LLOYD WRIGHT

American architect; founder of school of organic architecture. Born 1869 in Wisconsin; educated University of Wisconsin; practising in Chicago in 1893. Renowned, criticized, and admired for his independence of thought and strong personality. Architect of buildings of unique design and structure throughout the United States, Europe and Japan. At the age of 88 he planned a mile-high skyscraper for erection in Chicago. Founder of a cultural experiment in the arts, the non-profit organization entitled the Frank Lloyd Wright Foundation at Taliesin, Wisconsin (summer) and Taliesin West, Arizona (winter), which has about 40 apprentices.

It had always been a joy to meet Frank Lloyd Wright for a friendly talk (he is one of the world's best conversationalists), but this time, in 1954, we had serious business in hand. I think the old gentleman felt, as I did, that we might even be about to record him, himself, his thoughts, for posterity. This portrait might well be the image of the great architect observed by future generations. And a curious rapport seemed to exist among us all that afternoon. ∼ Wright was a little playful at first, however. Being surrounded at Taliesin West, in Arizona, by twenty-three of his disciples, he claimed to be outraged by my former portrait showing a cigarette in his hand. 'Brother Karsh,' he said, 'there are not many of us left. And yet you did this to me! I shall never live that portrait down because I never smoke.' I must have looked distressed at this charge of professional dishonesty for Mrs. Wright leaned towards me and whispered: 'Don't take Frank too seriously.' Then she raised her voice for all to hear: 'Silence, everybody! Let's put history right. When Karsh first photographed Frank, he not only drank but smoked. Since he gave up smoking he wants everybody to forget he ever indulged.' Wright gave his wife a sheepish smile and went on, hour after hour, to deliver a series of dicta on things in general without any prompting from me; these were taken down by a friend. ∼ 'Man is not at his best when he's aware of himself.' ∼ 'Literature tells about life; architecture *presents* men. Through the architecture of an age you reconstruct man by what he *presented* in his lifetime.' ∼ 'Genius—that's an appellation distrusted in the United States. The term arouses the suspicion of the people.' ∼ Wright seemed to tire after a while and remarked wearily: 'Brother Karsh is squeezing the last juice out of this orange—if there is any juice.' ∼ Soon he rallied himself to deliver a more important judgment. 'Democracy presents the prophecy of the superior man. Out of the common comes the uncommon. Only so can we justify our faith in democracy. It's superior to communism as it rises above the common. We should produce the superior man. We have not yet risen into the true state of human being—the perception of what we call "God." The perceptive artist is fulfilling the prophecy of the human being—waking the sense of beauty which is his birthright as a human. The Kingdom of God is within you. It lies in the great sense of *being*. The beautiful is a great sense of being. At the present stage of our development that sense of beauty is the most desirable state. Man is on tip-toe, reaching through feeling towards the stars as a God-like creation. Divinity is innate, not beyond the stars, but in our own souls. Most men are scrambling through life, ready always to snatch and run, thus cutting themselves off from divinity within. If I don't believe in the *now*, I can't believe in the hereafter.'

APPENDIX

Since the publication of my first book, FACES OF DESTINY, *many professional and amateur photographers have been kind enough to suggest that any succeeding volume should contain an appendix of technical data, a description of my photographic methods. I publish the facts below with some reluctance because, in my opinion, such data should be taken only as a general guide and should not be considered as a set of concrete rules. They will be useless and even misleading to some other photographers. I can only say that they work satisfactorily for me, or at least that they are the best methods I have been able to devise for my own work after long years of trial and error.*

To what follows must be added, of course, a generous measure of human understanding, at any rate a rough knowledge of psychology, and the experience with both camera and people which comes only out of long, hard practice. I have never standardized my technique and am constantly experimenting, taking advantage of the many new materials being offered to photographers today.

CAMERA

I nearly always use an 8×10 inch camera and employ a full range of Ektar lenses from 127 mm. to 14 inches. Occasionally I use a 4×5 inch view camera or a Rolleiflex. I also have a 35 mm. Leica and a Kodak Retina Reflex, one for black-and-white photography and one for colour.

FILM

It has been difficult to standardize on a special film for my portraits, but I use Kodak Portrait Pan, Super Panchro Type B, and Super XX. For 35 mm. I use Tri-X and for Rolleiflex, Verichrome. When working with electronic lights I avoid the use of fast emulsion film. I always develop my own film, usually in DK 50, and supervise the making of the 'master' print.

LIGHTING

In my studio, under established conditions, my preference is still for Tungsten lighting—floods and spots.

Invariably I use electronic lights when working abroad, or on location, and 90 per cent of my work is done outside my studio. My electronic flash equipment consists of four units of 200 watt seconds each. Sometimes I use only one in conjunction with available light.

In organizing my lighting I begin by establishing my 'key,' or main light. Only then do I organize my auxiliary or fill-in-light.

EXPOSURE

I read exposure meters, both Norwood and Weston, periodically (but only if I think the reading coincides with what I feel it should be). This applies to black-and-white photography. The exception is colour work, where I use sheet Ektachrome Daylight and Ektachrome Daylight roll film. The exposure latitude in all forms of colour film is so limited that only when I am working under lighting conditions completely under my control, and with which I am familiar from long usage, do I rely on the physical rather than the photo-electric eye.

This book has been printed in the Netherlands by Joh. Enschedé en Zonen, Haarlem,
under the direction of the University of Toronto Press, on Héliomat paper
made by Office Français des Papiers Fiduciaires & Surfins, Paris.
The photographs have been reproduced by sheet-fed gravure
and the text by offset lithography. Types used
are Spectrum and Dubbele Augustijn
Open Kapitalen, both designed
by Jan van Krimpen.
Production editor:
Paul Arthur